*May River to Ocean inspire and serve your most awakened life! ♡ Katherine*

# River to Ocean

## Living in the Flow of Wakefulness

Katherine Jansen-Byrkit, MPH, LPC

Harbor Glow Publishing
Portland, Oregon

D1707373

Harbor Glow Publishing
0404 SW Pendleton St
Portland, Oregon 97239
www.HarborGlowPublishing.com

ISBN 9781733744904 (book)
ISBN 9781733744911 (ebook)

Cover & interior design:
Micah (MJ) Schwader at www.inspiredlifepublishing.com
Cover image: Loma Smith

Publisher's Cataloging-In-Publication Data
Jansen-Byrkit, Katherine, author.
    River to ocean: living in the flow of wakefulness / Katherine
  Jansen-Byrkit, MPH, LPC.
    Portland, Oregon: Harbor Glow Publishing, [2019]
    ISBN 9781733744904 (book) | ISBN 9781733744911 (ebook)
    LCSH: Jansen-Byrkit, Katherine--Mental health. | Mindfulness
  (Psychology) | Self-consciousness (Awareness) | Peace of mind. |
  Suffering--Psychological aspects.
    LCC BF637.M56 J36 2019 (print) | LCC BF637.M56 (ebook) |
  DDC 158.1/3--dc23
    Printed in the United States of America

"The beautifulness is everywhere!"

*~ Emma Jane Gillooley, age 5*

# Dedication

This book is dedicated to my children, for whom my deepest hope is to live an awakened life. I also offer these writings to all who are devoted to the path of embodied wakefulness.

# Gratitude

There are so many to acknowledge and thank for the influence they have had in my life, and directly in writing this book. First and foremost, my husband has been my greatest teacher. Gary, you set the tone for what I now understand as the Divine flowing within and all around us. Thank you to each of my children and their partners, who have been a rock for me with the deep and abiding love that we share.

To my other teachers: Tara Brach, Ph.D, Sri Ramana Maharshi, Gangaji, Richard Bach, Catherine Ingram, Devaji, Brene Brown, Gabrielle Roth, Byron Katie, David Richo, Stephen Levine, Pema Chodron, Sue Monk Kidd, Michael A Singer, Miguel Ruez, Dan Siegal, Oprah, Cheryl Strayed, Eckhart Tolle, Jon Kabot-Zinn, Thich Nhat Hanh, Elizabeth Lesser, and many others; such immense gratitude for your work and its availability to me.

In addition, a huge thank you to my clients, who have and continue to inspire my work and these writings. To my readers, thank you for holding my vulnerability as a new writer with such love, gentleness, and honesty. To those who have agreed to share their stories of wakefulness, this book would not be the same without your inspiring *Story from the field*. Appreciation also to my parents, sisters, and to those amazing soul sisters/brothers I travel with as friends; each of you have filled my heart, offering deep love through life's many dark corners and alleyways.

Finally, to my incredible coach and editor, MJ Schwader, you have traveled this path of *River to Ocean* with such support, enthusiasm, wisdom, and patience. I could not have done this without you.

To this amazing tribe I am so lucky to call my own, thank you, thank you, thank you.

# Table of Contents

# Foreword

*River to Ocean* is written in a tantalizing way, gently urging us to awaken to the inner truth that we are put here on this planet to live actively, fully engaged, and deeply committed to all aspects of ourselves: our mind, body, and spirit. The modern world offers a daily torrent of unpleasant, negative experiences, including, but not limited to, hate, violence, deceit, and selfishness. Much of our world seems to be greedy for power, status, money, and control, relentlessly seeking *more* – more possessions, more space, more time, more glamour, and more attention to our "specialness." In the world of "more is better," ironically, many of us feel starved for meaning in our lives, for a sense of genuine purpose, for a sense of calm and serenity.

*River to Ocean* is an exquisite work that invites all of us to move smoothly, gracefully, awkwardly, or stumbling – it doesn't matter how – into the flow of our inner being, our awareness of self…our own wakefulness. Doing so is the antidote to our craving for more personal value in our lives.

Katherine Jansen-Byrkit's work takes us on a spiritual journey of the soul, a deliberate deep dive into ourselves. The model of this book takes us step-by-step through the most important descriptions of what discovering and awakening to our inner selves is all about. The narrative then brings us to "Stories from the field"… people sharing their process of awakening to their inner selves. And finally, Katherine activates the process within ourselves with important questions and meditations designed to enhance and move us forward on our path of discovery.

With her accompaniment and guidance there is something very soothing, exciting, challenging, and yet comforting in this endeavor; we are guided along the flow of our inner process with the strength of commitment, clarity, focus, and perseverance that

Katherine offers throughout *River to Ocean*. With her wisdom and direction, along with our intuitive sense of discovery, we are led along the river current toward a greater consciousness, awareness, and embodied wakefulness…that is our Self.

David J. Kleber, Ph.D

Clinical Psychologist

# Introduction

It's spring as I write this introduction. Right now, the world is alive with sights, sounds, tastes, and smells that are readily available. For some, it is easier to feel "awake" with warm sunshine and the blissfulness of an open, blue sky, birds chirping in the morning, and the anticipation of the summer's gifts of campfires and starry nights. But to be awake through the moments and the seasons of your life when it is not easy to do so can be even more powerful. Imagine experiencing a sense of flow in your life, including when it is the dark of winter or you are having a dark night of the soul, when you feel cold or cold-hearted, when a loved one is angry or disappoints you, or perhaps you are in the early dawn of some type of hangover of regret: overindulging a substance, a relationship miss, or somehow being out of integrity. My hope for all of us is to discover the possibility of feeling awake when it really counts.

I sit each morning looking at the river before me, watching the current provide the clearest path to the ocean. This river contends with many things as it travels toward the sea but eventually finds its way. Living in the flow of wakefulness is like being the river, navigating the difficult terrain of your life as your most loving and conscious self with the current as your guide, not only when the waters of life are smooth but, even more, in the roughness of the rapids. This way of being is in contrast to floating mindlessly through life, getting stuck in eddies, or drifting great distances without knowing where you are or how you got there.

Wakefulness, as I am defining it, is the experience of living in deep relaxation, with an abiding connection to yourself and others, being fully present in each moment, while knowing yourself as part of something bigger, however you define that something.

This definition of wakefulness might seem idealistic, or even elusive; though if you pause right now and reread my description, my guess is that you have had moments when you were relaxed, connected, and present, as well as having felt part of something bigger than you. And as you will see, wakefulness does not mean denying your humanity. Instead, embracing your human self and life connects you to the flow of wakefulness within it.

♦

I have organized this book based on my healing journey, which began as an inside job. At 16 years old, almost 200 lbs., and actively suicidal, I could not begin to imagine being out of pain, much less the experience of wakefulness within it. But I had to wake up. To become alive, whole, and at peace meant moving toward the pain I carried and not away from it. I had to heal from what sourced my despair. I had to heal my body and stop the violence I was perpetrating onto it. I had to learn what being in a conscious relationship meant, with myself and within my relationships. Ultimately, I had to rediscover who I was. Most areas of my life were affected, so in waking up, much of my life needed to transform, in both my inner *and* my outer worlds.

As in my journey, I distinguish in the book between your inner world and your outer world. Within that framework, I identify nine *Aspects of Wakefulness*. Within each of these *Aspects*, I offer ideas for integration to make it your own in the section titled *Practice*. Then, I end with a splash of inspiration, offering real-life stories that bring each particular idea and *Aspect of Wakefulness* to life. The hope is that in understanding and transforming your inner world, you take that awakened self to the outer regions of your life.

*Aspect One* is about your relationship to yourself because these are the headwaters of your life. The rest builds from there, with each *Aspect* drawing upon the previous one. Though I encourage you to start at the beginning as a foundation for the rest of the book, feel free to start anywhere that compels you. *Aspects One* and *Seven* are the most substantial, both in ideas and length. Each *Aspect* is like an invitation to visit a different spot along the river. You can stand for a quick glimpse, or spread out a blanket and indulge fully in a picnic.

To get the most out of *Aspect One* in particular, I encourage you to go slowly and to take breaks. Reflect upon what you have read so that it can be fully and deeply absorbed. Know that in *Aspect One*, we dive right in, which feels very different than wading in slowly. Know also that this book may make you uncomfortable as much as it inspires you. You can trust that your discomfort is a sign that something meaningful is at hand.

♦

We live in an exciting time. Neurological research has offered an emerging awareness that you can alter your brain and forge new neural pathways over time. Repetition, practice, and a willingness to be uncomfortable are critical to this process of neurological change that ultimately leads to healing and transformation; change that can manifest as a new relationship to your body, healing from trauma, decreased anxiety and depression, healthier relationships, and spiritual aliveness. *River to Ocean* helps you move from awareness to integration, which is the process that creates and sustains real, permanent change.

Just like the river flows to the ocean, you are part of a greater whole, moving toward that vastness on your individual, precious path: your human life. My intention for you is to experience wakefulness as you navigate the waters of life, amidst adversity and alongside struggle, as you travel toward that expansiveness that is who you are and is yours to claim.

Finally, I offer these writings as *my* answers, not *the* answers. Some of you reading this book could write your version of it. Others are new to a portion or all of the ideas around wakefulness I present. My hope is that I strike a balance between those of you familiar with wakefulness and those of you who are not, and inspire all readers to affirm and explore wakefulness within his or her life. Ultimately, it is my intention for this book to be a handbook that you return to again and again.

*Katherine Jansen-Byrkit*

P.S. As you enjoy the *Stories from the Field* throughout *River to Ocean*, imagine your own stories coming to life. Visit www.HarborGlowPublishing.com where I invite you and others on the path of embodied wakefulness to share your inspiring stories.

# Part One

## The Inner World

# Aspect One
# Befriending You

"i am mine.
before i am ever anyone else's."

~ Nayyirah Waheed, Nejma

Welcome. You are about to begin a journey that will take you through wild rapids and calm swimming holes; an expedition of life that is already well on its way but can dramatically change as you travel with greater wakefulness and aliveness.

To begin, you must start with the most important relationship in your life: your relationship to yourself. Wakefulness means that you are friends with and friendly toward many things, most importantly yourself. Perhaps you already have a well-established relationship with yourself. You might even call it a friendship. But notice what happened when you read the words "Befriending You" in the title. If those words confirm what already exists, then this *Aspect* offers a deepening of that friendship. But if the words conjure up a sense of something missing, or worse, of a relationship that is far from friendly and even further from friendship, this *Aspect* was written especially for you. And you are not alone. Many of us have realized at a certain point in our lives that we needed to rebuild and repair our relationship to ourselves.

My first invitation to you is to make your relationship to yourself active, intentional, and chosen. Doing this is in contrast to a relationship that is passive, neglected, or non-existent. Taking this step by itself can be revolutionary. And beyond that, I invite you to be fierce in creating a loving, kind relationship. This action, too, can be transformative.

Later sections of this *Aspect* will help you with the quality of your relationship to yourself. But before we go there, the questions to ask are, "*Who* are you loving? *Who* are you befriending? *Who* are you?" When you ask the last question, if you are like most people, you have defined who you are by your name, life history, personality, and the multitude of choices and mistakes you've made. Maybe you have even explored your ancestry to learn more about yourself. But what if there's more? The point is that you may not have gotten as far as you can in contemplating "Who am I?"

I propose to you a possibility, one that is life-changing in its potential: you are much more than your human self. You are not just alive; you are aliveness. You are not only present; you are presence. You are not merely aware; you are awareness.

To help understand this possibility, imagine traveling upstream to the wellspring of your existence. Asking the question "Who am I?" takes you to where it all starts. When you arrive at the headwaters of the stream, at the source of your being, a truth awaits: that whatever sourced you *is* you. It lives and breathes as you.

This powerful realization means that beyond your name, history, personality, and choices, you are part of something much bigger than your individuality. What emerges from this discovery is a new, expanded sense of self; one that is boundless in nature, even though it is bound in a body and brought to life on your human journey. To say it directly, we can call this source of life "God", "higher power", "Consciousness", or "Love". If it is easier to go a more scientific route, perhaps you can define this source as the innate intelligence that has been explained by sages throughout history and verified by quantum physics. Ultimately, the words don't matter. What matters is the realization that you are innately part of what created you.

Back to our river metaphor, envision zooming out and gazing over a beautiful landscape filled with mountains and valleys, and throughout it all, flowing brooks, streams, and creeks. Zoom out so that you can see the headwaters of each, and the ocean that they all join. Notice how each river finds its way to the sea, some more easily than others and some that have many miles to traverse. Each one is connected to the sea, even when the ocean isn't visible with the bends and turns the river takes. Ultimately, they are all one; bound together in sameness by the water they share.

This vision is a reflection of you. You are the headwaters and the river and the ocean all at the same time. The river is not just the river. You are not just your human life.

A part of you may already recognize this. Perhaps you have had the sneaking suspicion that you are more than your personhood. This idea, whether you have felt inklings of it before or if it is a new prospect, can generate many feelings, from exhilaration to terror. Who doesn't love the idea of being connected to something big and something good? And it can be very appealing to get off the hamster wheel of living the "me" story, potentially ending the perpetual search for who you are.

But it can also be overwhelming and a bit disorienting to define who you are as part of something vast and unfamiliar. If you feel overwhelmed or disoriented, imagine it this way: instead of losing yourself in the vastness, think of it as being held by the limitlessness that also lives within you.

For some people, there is a sense of loss when adopting an expanded definition of who they are. Feelings of grief can arise if you think it is about giving up "you". But that is not what you are doing. Redefining who you are builds on what is already true and doesn't have to threaten it. Instead, you get to stop living from a limited view of yourself. Know that your human experience, your life, and your sense of self are invaluable. Each will always be a part of who you are.

The metaphor of you as a river can help when you experience a sense of losing yourself. Each river is unique, yet part of a bigger whole. While every river is one of a kind and always changing, what doesn't vary is its innate connection to the ocean. Imagine miles upstream the rocks and seashells found on the riverbed – a part of the sea within its banks. You are like the river, with life's treasures swirling in you, invited to celebrate your individuality without discounting the vastness of which you are a part.

Your awakened self knows you as this expanded definition of self. As this idea takes hold, the next step is to ask how well it translates into real life? For most, the answer is, not so well. While thrilling as a concept, you might be stuck living in the old paradigm of who you thought you were.

One of the reasons for being caught in the old sense of self is your ego, the part of you that has known itself as distinct from others. In defining your ego, it is the sense of "I" that is and has been an essential part of you. It serves to create a sense of personhood necessary for healthy human development. But when the feeling of personhood and individuality is in direct opposition to the innate connection to others and the source of life, it is the opposite of wakefulness.

Ego is best known by how it operates, which is mainly in fear; it is the part of you that feels inferior or superior, that wants to blame others and shies away from accountability. It is the part of you that always wants to look good, be right, thrives in competition, and can sulk when not getting its way.

Though the ego can interfere with living wakefully, it is essential to understand the role of your ego in creating your initial sense of self. In childhood, to experience optimal development as a person, it is crucial for you to have a sense of "me" to evolve as a person and to understand your place in the world. This important process builds what is called "ego strength". Athena Staik, Ph.D. defined this term as "*a cultivated resiliency or strength of our core sense of self, the extent to which we learn to face and grow from challenging events or persons in our lives in ways that strengthen our relationships with our self and others and enrich our lives with meaning. Our ego-strength is an integral part of our psycho-social-emotional and cultural development and forms our sense of self in relation to self and others around you."*

Additionally, both in childhood and as an adult, your ego serves as a protective force keeping you from experiencing pain or threat. As a youngster, your ego developed defenses that helped you cope with what was happening. For all of us, but particularly for those who have experienced trauma or loss, that protection was vital for survival. As an adult, those defenses continue to exist as a way of protecting you from perceived harm. Consider how amazing it is that there exists a part of you always ready and able to protect you. Without your ego, you may not have survived many of your life experiences as well as you did.

The problem arises when the danger has passed, but the protective force lives on, often in the form of defenses such as aggression, avoidance, or detachment. Though defenses aim to keep you safe, when there isn't a real threat, they stop you from being fully authentic and feeling alive and limit your capacity to connect deeply – to yourself and to others. Defenses keep you from being relaxed and trap you in the past. The distance they create between you and the perceived threat is a way to prevent you from re-experiencing old pain. That protective distance means, however, that you are not living as your awakened self. Remember the definition of living in the flow of wakefulness is being relaxed, connected, and present. In the protective posture of the ego, you are likely anxious, feeling disconnected from yourself and others, and potentially reacting from the past or the future.

So to live as this newly defined "you" means helping the ego, this protective part of you, be at ease. Imagine that it's like a warrior who won't put down the shield long after the battle has ceased. It's scary to be without protection, which is why it is so important to appreciate that your ego has served you in this way. As you imagine gently dropping the armor, you let go of the shield that ultimately keeps you in separation and fear. Letting go gets easier when you understand the illusion that maintains the armor.

Your ego has operated in the illusion of not being connected or enough. From the standpoint of your awakened self, you don't have to be or do anything to be connected. You already are. You don't have to do or be anything more, because you are already enough. What a relief to relax into what is already true. Take a deep breath right now and read that sentence again. As your awakened self, you get to relax into what is real and already yours: connection and wholeness.

Given that you are inherently connected and complete, a question can arise for those who have been enjoying the path of personal evolution: "Where does the quest for making personal changes fit in?" It still has a place, but it becomes more about *how* you evolve. You aren't necessarily *changing* who you are, but instead *deepening* your sense of self, dropping the outdated, limited version. Your best and most sustainable changes then happen as part of living in the flow of wakefulness and don't come from fear or the illusion of disconnection or inadequacy.

For many, personal changes originate from an old idea of who he or she is: not good enough, imperfect, and broken. Starting from that place feels bad, often shameful, and therefore the environment of change is a negative one. If you start there, the changes are more challenging to make and sustain: "I have to exercise because my body is flawed." "I have to change my driving because everyone hates being with me in the car." Changes like that are good ideas but feel awful because there is judgment.

Instead, envision inviting change as part of wakefulness. Imagine yourself transforming and moving toward what is expansive and pleasant and not away from something bad: "I change my driving because I am connected to other drivers as well as the people in the car with me." "I take care of my body because I love and cherish it, not because I loathe it." Change comes about in an environment of love and ease, which not only feels better but the changes themselves are more likely to be maintained. In this process, you shift from self-judgment to self-love.

As you take in these words, relaxing into innate wholeness and connectedness and inviting change from a place of love rather than fear, the next piece can be integrating your awakened self amidst your day-to-day existence. This shift can be challenging. Many life experiences can trigger a response from your old sense of self, from the place of separation, fear, judgment, and illusion. When this happens, your job is to gently remind yourself of who you are: aliveness, presence, and awareness…boundless. Being kind and patient with yourself is crucial as you learn to live day-to-day from this new awareness of who you are.

I close this section with a beautiful piece, illuminating where we meet when living as our awakened selves:

> *Out beyond the ideas of wrong doing and right doing, there is a field;*
> *I'll meet you there.*
>
> ~Rumi

## Practice

- Spend a few quiet moments with the idea that what sourced you *is* you; notice how that idea feels, emotionally and in your body.

- Consider a daily journal practice that focuses on where and how often your ego is in charge, without judgment. Be curious and pay attention to the impact your focus provides; are you less in your ego when you are more aware of it?

- Reflect on your response to words like God, Consciousness, higher power, etc. Ask yourself if you are reacting to some conditioning around that word rather than embracing what it might reflect. If so, ask yourself further what word works for you. For many of us, the word "God" is loaded. My personal preference is the word "Love".

- Begin to identify those in your life that seem to have less ego; maybe you see them as collaborative versus competitive or taking responsibility versus blaming others. Talk to them about what you see.

- Read books that focus on ego work. Good books to start with are *You Are Not What You Think* by David Richo or *A New Earth* by Eckhart Tolle.

- Listen to the song "Pilgrim" by Enya.

*Stories from the field . . .*

Gary might have told you long ago that he knew who he was. Like so many of us, his sense of identity was based on being a strong individual with goals and aspirations. The eldest of six children and raised in a loving but traditionally Christian household, Gary's sense of self worked – until it didn't. What our culture and his upbringing had told him was shattered into pieces when he was exposed to the idea that he was intrinsically part of God, not separate. Much unfolded from this profound realization, including leaving the seminary, forging a path of personal growth, and adopting spiritual practices. Bit by bit, year by year, Gary has grown to embody his sense of self as expansive and connected to the source from which he came. That doesn't mean that he never gets caught in what he once believed. The conditioning was intense, and the culture he lives in is powerful in keeping him trapped in his old sense of self. But an important thing happened. Gary had a glimpse of who he really is. That glimpse launched a lifetime commitment to deepen and embody his true self. He still has, of course, his name, a career and family, an ego to contend with, and certain ways of being. But Gary is not solely defined by any of that and lives more and more in the freedom that is the gift of knowing who he is.

◆

Moving downstream with an expanded sense of who you are, we begin exploring the landscape of your inner world.

## Your Inner Witness

Right now, there is a part of you that is sitting quietly, completely relaxed and at ease, observing what is unfolding without judgment or reaction. This part of you is your inner witness. Unaffected by the world's ups and downs, the stories of your mind, or the history you have, your inner witness is at peace through all of it. This powerful part of your existence can help you live wakefully in your inner world. Delightfully, your inner witness is unaffected by whether you have an awareness of it or not. It merely exists, paying attention to what is happening, no matter how big or small the experience. Think of it as the eyes of the expansive presence within you.

Without an inner witness, intense emotions or the wild stories of the mind can seem to swallow you up. There is a certain truth in this since your internal experience can be intense. But even when you think you are lost in the trance of your mind, your inner witness is still apart from it, tracking what is happening. In accessing your inner witness, your perspective can shift from "I am my experience" to "I am having an experience." Or in a more specific example, "I am my depression" or "There is only depression" to "I am experiencing depression."

That shift in perspective means that you get to enjoy a sense of calm with the small but profound amount of buffering that your inner witness offers. When overwhelmed by an experience, it is easy to shut down, so any amount of cushioning is enormous in terms of staying present.

Even in cases of severe trauma or loss, where the brain goes "offline" to cope, the inner witness is still aware of what's happening. This essential process provides a sense of safety by disassociating with the experience when the resources are not available, while the inner witness puts the event into a memory bank until you are ready.

When you or I inevitably experience frightening or painful events as we traverse the peaks and valleys of life, our inner witness can be incredibly helpful. Putting our attention on this part and not the painful or scary experience offers relief. Doing this doesn't mean that we are avoiding what is happening within. Our inner witness simply makes it easier to get through. For those who have experienced significant trauma or loss earlier in life, the ability to access an inner witness helps in being able to deal with old pain. Our inner witness is not the pain itself, and therefore it is easier to face pain without becoming overwhelmed.

To access your inner witness, start with paying attention to the part of you that is aware of and tracking your experience, whether that experience is your thoughts, feelings, sensations, images, or intuition. At first, this can be elusive. But keep at it, and over time you will discover that your inner witness is not *having* the experience; it is *noticing* it.

Working with my own inner witness is unfolding as I write this book. I will share part of this story now, and the rest of it in *Aspect Three, Mindfulness: Working with Pain*. Recently diagnosed with a condition that requires life-long phlebotomies, I had to put my inner witness into practice. My significant fear of needles, along with the lightheadedness I felt when dealing with them, meant that

I had to come to terms with an anxiety-producing experience that I initially resisted but ultimately will face the rest of my life.

So here's how it goes on a good phlebotomy day when I can engage my inner witness: when I am sitting in the chair, waiting for the needle poke and catheter insertion, I start the process of accessing my inner witness. I focus on the part of me that is observing the experience and not on the fears and body sensations I am having. That little bit of space is colossal in shifting the experience from one I resist to one that is bearable. I still feel the fear and the sensations, but over time, my inner witness has gotten stronger, and therefore those feelings are less intense. With my inner witness, I can sit in the chair, with the catheter in, working with and not against the sensations and feelings, aware but not swallowed up in the experience.

There is one last gift that your inner witness offers you: objectivity, which in turn helps you to be honest with yourself. Self-awareness grows with your ability to see yourself and what is happening most accurately. With the increased self-awareness your inner witness offers, you are gifted with a great set of binoculars on the river, providing a clear and accurate view.

Before diving further into the waters of self-awareness, explore the inner witness practice ideas below.

## Practice

1. Notice right now something within you – a thought, feeling, or sensation. Who or what is noticing this? See if you can have the experience, with the awareness of noticing it at the same time. I call this dual awareness, which means that you are both aware of the thing itself and the part of you aware of it.

2. Take this perspective of dual awareness, of accessing your inner witness while having an experience, into your day. For

example, taste the flavor of your morning tea as you also notice yourself tasting it. Do this with as many experiences as you can to get a good sense for how your inner witness is always working.

3.  As you bring stronger attention to your inner witness, ask, "Is the part of me noticing what is happening stressed or at peace?" Likely, your inner witness is at peace and relaxed, which aligns with your relaxed and at ease awakened self.

## *Stories from the field* . . .

Lily came to see me for severe anxiety that debilitated her life. Anxious thoughts and a constantly activated nervous system tormented her, in addition to having deep sadness and tears for how affected she was. Trying to "white knuckle" it to get through life didn't work and worsened her anxiousness. When I offered a different way of working with her anxiety, she was very receptive. So I encouraged her to witness her experience. Staying committed to observing what was happening, while being anxious at the same time, was difficult. At first, she barely noticed anything except her anxiety. But over time, her capacity to witness her fear in a non-judgmental way provided a welcome shift. In witnessing her internal experience, she turned toward it; her inner witness gave her just enough space to breathe easier. Since then, Lily has experienced a profound change and great relief, not because the anxiety has gone away but because Lily can be present with it in a way like never before. She has found that now, when feeling anxious, her attention on her inner witness calms her down. And even better, Lily knows that regardless of the inevitable moments of anxiety that will arise again, her inner witness is the friend that will be there in the future when she needs it.

# Self-Awareness

You have undoubtedly met wonderful people who are completely unaware of themselves. Perhaps you have been one of those people at some point. To become aware can be painful in that it requires the courage and strength to be honest with yourself. So the question naturally arises: why become more self-aware? There are many answers to that crucial question. Mostly, it is only in becoming aware of what is true that you can attend to what might need attention. Becoming self-aware means breaking out of a trance, and what follows is the ability to have choices that you did not have before.

For the unaware person, life is run by patterns, many that are based in injury or traced to poor modeling from parents, or from deferring to an outside source. Patterns can also be habits that become entrenched over time. Being self-aware by seeing repeated tendencies and what drives them offers the possibility of becoming free from their effects. A great example is someone who has defined themselves as an extrovert. If the extrovert looks deeply at what seems to be a personality trait and a pattern of behavior, they may find that their extroversion is actually a need for attention that was absent in childhood.

Your willingness and interest in being self-aware is the first step in becoming so. Your freedom from the control of any particular pattern is like waking up from sleepwalking. Self-awareness can be like a welcome splash of cold water that breaks you out of a trance.

Consider the following:

- Do characteristics of your personality align with your awakened self?

- Are you aware of any injuries or fears that drive you?

- Do you feel like you are walking around in a daze, on autopilot, controlled by patterned ways of being?

If you give a resounding "Yes!" to any of these questions, consider what comes next. Something needs to change to break out of the pattern. Increasing self-awareness often leads to change, so make sure you are ready. Whether it is the discipline to break a long-standing habit or the deep work of healing an injury, making and sustaining change is hard work. Remember to invite change based on the idea of living as your awakened self. And though engaging in a change process may ask much of you, know that it is well worth the effort. You are shedding an old coat that you've outgrown, free of the tight-fitting fabric and able to move without constriction.

Specific patterns in your life may have started with somebody else's injury or fear. Breaking behaviors that have existed for generations is motivating. Your freedom is gifted to those who come after you in a "pay it forward" kind of way. You can ask yourself whether or not you took on a way of being without a second glance, unaware of the impact it would have on your quality of life or living as your awakened self.

I'll give you a concrete example. Picture a family that lives in isolation from others. Though close to each other, they have very little social connection with the outside world. Neither parent takes time to deepen and enjoy adult friendships. Somewhere along the line, the parents or those who came before them began living apart from others. Over time, that became the norm. Children raised with this way of being can then minimize the role of friendship in their adult life. They aren't being shown how to maintain close adult relationships amidst many other priorities and responsibilities. They might not even know the importance of it for their well-being.

Another example is a family that has a ton of love, but their expression of that love is repressed. They may also be repressed in expressing many other emotions, all because somebody or something long ago encouraged repression of love and feelings. When an absence of emotional expression continues over generations, family members learn to hide their feelings, unable to express what is in their heart. If you are in that type of family, it is nothing short of heroic to break free of a generational culture of repressed emotion.

In terms of generational patterns, there are those who have what is called "generational guilt" or feelings of guilt or shame for acts they did not commit that are carried forward generation after generation. Asking the question, "What did *I* do wrong?" is essential to be free of inherited guilt. Becoming free does not remove the opportunity to contribute on behalf of wrongs that have occurred by others but doing so will be without a personal sense of guilt. Instead, contributions come from a place of love.

These are examples of looking honestly at ways of being through becoming more self-aware. Your willingness, interest, and ability to ask the tough questions, such as, "Does this way of being reflect my awakened self?" or "Am I standing in a long line of learned behavior?" is a huge step toward living in the flow of wakefulness. Whatever you do with your newfound self-awareness, the most important thing is to recognize that without it, you are unable to make different choices.

Beyond the reflective questions above, here are some additional ideas that can help you to deepen self-awareness.

## Practice

1.  Ask yourself, "Am I aware of my history, patterns, and personality? How have these each impacted my life and my

relationships? How current is that impact, and am I willing and ready to make any necessary changes so that I am living as my awakened self? Do any of my personality traits feel permanent, and, if so, do they align with my awakened self?"

All of these questions are big and may be best explored with the help of a therapist. If you take them on yourself, I encourage you to take one at a time.

Also, consider journaling daily with any question that speaks to you. Observe your progress in how you think about these questions and apply your thinking to your daily life.

2. Dive into your personal history, since many patterns arise from childhood experiences. In building self-awareness, understanding what you did and didn't get when you were growing up is important. Acknowledging what you find is even more critical. Many feel disloyal to their hard-working parents if they admit that they didn't get everything they needed. What I offer is this: parents generally do the best they can with what they have. Further, most parents try to improve in some way upon the previous generation, or at the very least, repeat the good stuff. In times past, there was much less information and support available for parents. Even with the most conscious and involved parent, it is nearly impossible to give a child everything they need. This part of your personal work is to accept the limitations of your parents and get on with the business of understanding what children need, and what was and was not available to you.

3. As I suggested in *Practice* idea #1, for a full exploration of your history, consider inviting a professional into the process. Having the help of a trained and seasoned psychotherapist who

knows the questions to ask and who has a background in child development can be quite enlightening. Conducting a history of your childhood with a therapist can help you learn what children need developmentally, and the impact if those needs remain unmet. Then, together, you can explore how your childhood circumstances and experiences did or did not meet those needs.

4.  Commit to transcending your patterns and healing any injury or pain that sources them. Though it may be obvious that you would intend to do so, making a clear commitment takes your efforts to a new level. Also, be open to the idea that parts of your personality are not really you but instead are the result of some form of conditioning. The exploration of your childhood experiences can show how circumstances and events shaped who you thought you were and how you coped as a child, potentially using those same coping strategies and defenses today in a way that no longer serves you.

    Remember that although your childhood pain was long ago, your ego, in the form of your defenses, is still trying to prevent further suffering. But your defenses and strategies also give rise to the patterns and personality that you have always thought defined you. In living as your awakened self, you must break the patterns that conflict with who you really are. Moving toward the pain that has sourced your patterns is no easy feat. The next section offers more on working with inner pain.

5.  Integrate your insights into behavioral changes, perhaps even before you do the emotional work of resolving the pain that drives any of your patterns. The great undoing of patterns and traits of personality often involves changing habits. While this can be uncomfortable, it is a crucial part of living as your

awakened self. Patterns have and can make you feel safe. It is important to recognize, however, that what kept you safe has become unsafe, since it imprisons you in an old way of being. What is safe, even though it does not feel comfortable, is breaking free from those patterns and traits of personality that are not you. I offer this as a new mantra:

*What feels unsafe is safe.*
*And what feels safe is keeping me from living as my awakened self.*

## Stories from the field ...

Michael is learning about self-awareness the hard way. For years, he has been unaware of his inner pain and the impact of the patterning that arose from that pain. Michael kept hitting a wall in life, so to speak, trying to be happy, and to be connected to himself, his wife, and his children. He had not been aware that his pattern of internalizing what he feels and what he wants was keeping him from his longed-for happiness. Michael had unmet needs he was unaware of – in his case, not getting enough positive recognition as a child. As he sought acknowledgment in his adult life to make up for what he didn't get in childhood, his choices for attention outside of his marriage created betrayal and injury. By completing his childhood history and while looking long and hard at his current choices, Michael has begun to crack open a new awareness. The experience has been both exciting and frightening; it hurts, and it feels good at the same time to finally have a sense of what has been happening. With self-awareness, he has begun to move forward in his life, which includes healing the little boy inside who didn't get what he needed. Now, Michael can make choices from a place of awareness and clarity, increasingly free from the patterns and pain that trapped him.

# Healing Our Brokenness: Path vs. Pathology

As you travel downstream, enjoying a more definite sense of who you are, with increased self-awareness around your patterns and perhaps a glimpse of where they may have started, you've likely come upon the rougher waters of inner pain.

In the practice section above, you got closer to these waters in your commitment to transcend any tendencies that keep you from living as your awakened self. As I said before, beyond any pattern that is driven by habit, many patterns at their core are sourced by pain. As you enter the waters of dealing with pain, especially if this is unfamiliar territory, you are not alone if you feel like you have to tighten your life vest. Saying yes to tuning in to inner pain is a big deal because, of course, what hurts, hurts. But to heal your pain is to feel it as it becomes unlocked and released. Many people go right up to the edge but don't take the plunge. They identify what hurts and leave it at that. Diving into this work, it can be helpful to have a positive framework in which to work.

The best frame I can offer is the good that is inherent in pain and suffering. First, the experience of pain and suffering serves to build resiliency as you evolve and learn life lessons. Further, pain is universal, and whatever the nature of pain and suffering, the bends and twists of your river journey, no one escapes this part of being human. Knowing you are not alone helps you feel the innate connection you have with others. Finally, in terms of the good pain can bring, your ability to truly empathize with another depends on your willingness to feel your pain.

As humans, each of us responds to pain in ways that are adaptive and healing, and sometimes in ways that are not. Often, those responses are the symptoms that become criteria for diagnosis and treatment in our medical system. For example, in my case, depression, food addiction, and an eating disorder were all linked to the divorce in my family.

Initially, a diagnosis can be very useful to understand a set of symptoms and to direct the process of treatment. But when a diagnosis becomes how you define yourself, it stops being helpful, kind of like how the ego gives you a limited definition of your self. What was important information to assist in treatment for symptoms can become a permanent reality about who you believe you are. This is troubling since the research is exploding with new possibilities around specific diagnoses. Some diagnostic conditions that were understood to be permanent are not. Unfortunately, for many, the damage was already done when a response to trauma or loss was packaged into a diagnosis that became part of the person's identity.

This scenario is in contrast to a different possibility, where a diagnosis is a reflection of a response to pain, loss, or trauma, and is positively affected by treatment. Over time, and as healing occurs, symptoms decrease, and criteria for the initial diagnostic may no longer be true. The following reflects this shift: what starts as "I *am* my anxiety disorder" changes to "I *have* an anxiety disorder" that might someday become "I had an anxiety disorder" and could ultimately become "I experience anxiety at times."

Turning human pain and suffering into pathology does more than mess with your identity. A sense of separation and being different can follow your diagnosis. When and if this happens, your sense of worth can be hugely impacted because being different can translate into feeling less somehow. This impact is so unfortunate, when, in fact, differences are simply a reflection of human diversity; each of us is the unique river that we are.

So here is the radical reframe. Your pain, including any diagnosis that you may have received, is part of your path. That's it. It's just part of your journey. Lean into these words and notice how you feel. As you learn to appreciate that pain has intrinsic good, as highlighted above, it gets easier to trust that your pain has been an essential part of your path. Ask yourself, "Has my pain been pathologized and did I internalize it as part of my identity?" and "What happens if I see my pain and suffering as an important part of my path?"

As we wrap up this section, I offer this: your pain is part of who you are as it reflects your human journey, your uniqueness, and your capacity to heal. If you can welcome your pain as part of the river that you are, it no longer defines, controls, or separates you.

I will spend time discussing working with inner pain as we explore *Mindfulness* further ahead. Reframing your pain as part of your path versus pathology is a great start. Below are ideas that can also help.

## Practice

1.  Reflect upon what labels or diagnosis that have ever been applied to you (or you have given yourself). Does the diagnosis feel like it means something is wrong with you and that you are broken somehow? And if so, does it feel permanent? Does the diagnosis feel like it defines you? Take your reflections into a journaling process.

2.  Ask yourself further, are you willing to change your relationship to the diagnosis or label?

    Here's an example: I was diagnosed with an eating disorder. It had always felt like who I was. As I've shifted away from identifying with it as a way of defining myself, I see that my eating disorder was a coping strategy for my pain and fear, a way to control something when my life felt out of control.

Even though it will be a lifetime of recovery, through changing my relationship to food, as well as managing the old thoughts and feelings that arise, I know the eating disorder is not who I am; I am not this diagnosis. In hindsight, I can understand and even celebrate that this way of coping with my pain and my recovery are essential pieces of my journey. The next practice idea builds on this.

3.  Now plunge into the deepest part – the recognition that your pain was not only a part of your path but also what you needed to become more conscious. Your willingness to see your suffering in this way transforms any sense of your pathology around your pain. Welcome your pain, as it is part of living as your awakened self. In the above example, in seeing my eating disorder as pain, and healing as part of the process of waking up, I learned to cherish, rather than harm my body. The truth is that my ability to tune into my body is better than it would have been if my eating disorder and recovery had not happened.

## Stories from the field . . .

Robert was diagnosed with Bipolar Disorder long ago. He not only believed the diagnosis, which was accurate at a particular time, he also felt the illness could never significantly change, which was inaccurate at some level. Mostly, he thought that his diagnosis was who he was. The thoughts, *This is who I am, I cannot trust myself with my emotions*, and especially, *I am incapable of having a successful romantic relationship*, haunted him. Over time, I have watched him, session after session, and month after month, challenge the premise that this is who he is. I have seen him confront the illusion that he cannot be free of his thoughts, and that how he had defined himself was unchangeable. As he redefined who he is, what is true, and faced his inner emotions, Robert has transformed. His Bipolar Disorder is part of him but less and less so. It is certainly not all of him. He is discovering that with the personal work he is doing, he knows that there will be even more transformation. If you were to sit with Robert, as I am privileged to do, you would see that there is a sense of lightness in him that wasn't there before. His walls are down, and he remains hopeful even on the most challenging of days. He has changed his relationship with himself and his relationship with his diagnosis. He is free from those thoughts about himself that were untrue and have been a glass ceiling in his life. During our work together, a relationship ended. For the first time in his life, he did not fall apart, did not experience emotions beyond what he could handle, and mostly, did not experience the breakup as evidence that he is incapable of a healthy relationship. Robert's Bipolar Disorder brought him into this work, which began a journey that may not have occurred without his original diagnosis. He knows in no uncertain terms that his pain was part of his path and necessary for him to heal and grow.

## You are the Beautiful River: Intrinsic Worth

Being enough. Feeling worthy. What a powerful idea and phrase. But are these words your words? More importantly, are they your truth? Could your imperfect, gnarly river be just as good, as beautiful, and as important as all of the other rivers?

In the previous section, you were invited to reframe your inner pain as part of your path. In terms of the pain itself, that may have landed you square in the middle of the heartache of feeling unworthy. Since most of us live in a culture that defines worthiness in terms of looks, accomplishment, or social status, it is common to struggle when worth is based on conditions. Pause for a moment and consider what you got in terms of the message you received from your parents and the world outside of your family. If you didn't hear that you are innately worthy, you are in the company of many others. The idea of worthiness, of being enough just the way you are, is one of the most important messages to receive in childhood. Your parents may not have been equipped to offer a message they themselves never received.

There are also those who find themselves in their adult life needing to claim their worth on their own, even if they *were* given that message as children. It can be confusing if you have been told or believed that you were enough but still struggle. Struggling with self-esteem makes sense given that we live in a culture that operates on conditional worth. Ultimately, claiming your innate worth is so powerful because you can give it to yourself.

I often find myself describing this essential part of being happy and whole to my clients: the idea of worthiness based on *innate* value, not on achievement, how we look, where we live, or how much money we have. For the majority of people that I have met and worked with, I rarely find someone who got the message of intrinsic worth. I ask those clients who are parents, "Do your children have innate value and intrinsic worth?" I always hear a resounding "Yes!" It's bewildering to me that the same folks who don't believe in their intrinsic worth, believe absolutely in their children's innate value. So then, of course, it becomes, "Why not you? If it is true for your child, how can it not be true for you?"

To dive a little deeper, I want you to notice how the idea of intrinsic worth for yourself feels; worth that includes your fallibility and your imperfections, no matter what is happening or has ever happened – the good, the bad, and the ugly. So take a moment, perhaps with your eyes closed, and see what shows up in emotions, body sensations, and images. Use your inner witness to see what happens when you sit with this idea.

Now, consider the opposite: the idea that your worth is changeable and has to be earned. Life events such as losing your job or someone leaving you, which are already upsetting, are debilitating because they are attached to your worthiness and value as a human being. Again, take a moment to take this in, and notice what shows up as an image, emotions, or bodily sensation.

The little experiment that you just did is a great place to start cultivating your sense of intrinsic worth. Sitting with worthiness, and potentially feeling the relief and joy that ensues, inspires the shift. Sitting with the feeling of unworthiness, and likely feeling shame and some form of despair can also be motivating because it doesn't feel good. The bottom line is to live in the knowledge that your intrinsic value is with you as you travel through space and time. No matter what is happening, your worth is not on the line. Ever. Period. You get to wake up every day with nothing to prove.

For most of us, this shift is revolutionary. It doesn't mean that life will not be upsetting or shake you to your core from time to time because job loss does happen, as does relationship change. With intrinsic worth, however, you have immunity from the despair, shame, fear, and devastation associated with feeling unworthy due to life events unfolding as they do; this is especially helpful in terms of how you feel about your mistakes. From a place of intrinsic worth, instead of feeling bad about yourself, you are free to use your mistakes as the teachings they are meant to be.

As part of claiming your intrinsic worth, focus on the **truth** of who you are. Your new, expanded definition of you is something grand and vast, so now your worth can be just as magnificent. By defining yourself as part of something innately good, you are intrinsically that same goodness. Your human fallibility and personal life events are merely part of being the beautiful, unique river that is you. As your awakened self, you are free from the idea of not being enough, understanding that it was all a big misunderstanding. It was only your mind that believed you were not enough. Thankfully, your awakened self has always known the truth.

Most of us love this idea and happily welcome it into our new way of thinking. Unfortunately, that isn't always enough to produce an embodied experience of *knowing* yourself as worthy. To do so, it helps to see whether or not you have feelings of unworthiness. Look for evidence in the form of needing to prove yourself to others. Making this inquiry is like detective work. When you find evidence of attempts to *feel good enough*, then you are likely to discover *not feeling good enough* underneath.

Once you see attempts to prove your worth, you may notice a dance between the underlying feeling of unworthiness and your ego's response in the form of attempts to refute it. The whole thing begins with the starting premise that "I am unworthy" followed by attempts to disprove this belief. Perhaps the attempt looks like taking a high-level job that you don't want in a relentless striving for achievement, or always having to look good. Maybe it is making sure you always have a relationship. It could be as subtle as comparing yourself to everyone else's IQ, leading you to mask your feelings of inadequacy by behaving as if you are smarter and superior.

For a while, "I have worth because I've proven it" works. But what happens when you lose the high-level job, your accomplishments aren't recognized, someone leaves you, or you experience the effects of aging? Your reprieve from the feeling of unworthiness is over, as your worth seems to dissolve right before your eyes. The unbearable sense of worthlessness and other emotions, such as shame and despair, drive new attempts to disprove unworthiness as the dance goes on and on.

Thankfully, seeing the cycle is the start of changing it, and builds on embracing the *idea* of intrinsic worth. Imagine a life free from the anxiety that accompanies self-worth gained and lost on the roller coaster of life. But gaining freedom from the cycle is easier said than done because your mind and belief system can work against that. The wild thing is that the mind searches for confirmation of its beliefs, even though a belief like "I am unworthy" causes such misery. Your mind looking for confirmation is called "confirmation bias". It will interpret life in such a way as to *affirm* your existing beliefs. So while your ego is busy trying to disprove the idea that you are unworthy, your mind is seeking evidence of its truth.

As you focus on the practice ideas offered below, be brave. Claiming your intrinsic worth may be the most important thing you ever do. Imagine that it is likely as simple as this: your sense of unworthiness comes down to a *lie that a child believed*. This part of you, perhaps this confused child within you, only needs someone to tell the truth. And that someone is you.

Below is a beautiful poem that captures intrinsic worth:

*'as you are.' says the universe.*
*'after…' you answer.*
*'as you are.' says the universe.*
*'before…' you answer.*
*'as you are.' says the universe.*
*'when…' you answer.*
*'as you are.' says the universe.*
*'how…' you answer.*
*'as you are.' says the universe.*
*'why…' you answer.*
*'because you are happening now. right now. right at this moment and your happening is beautiful. the thing that both keeps me alive and brings me to my knees. you don't even know how breathtaking you are; as you are.' says the universe through tears.*
*— as you are | you are the prayer ~ Nayyirah Waheed, Nejma*

## Practice

1. To build self-awareness around your sense of worth, reflect upon the answer to the following question: "Do I believe myself to be worthy without conditions?"

2. As you choose to see yourself as having intrinsic worth, focus on your definition of who you are. If you are doing the work of redefining yourself as part of the whole, part of something good, then experiencing yourself as having intrinsic worth will become easier.

3. To become fully aware of any sense of unworthiness, begin to look for the dance of the ego seeking to prove your worth. Also, look for the mind interpreting events as evidence of your unworthiness (confirmation bias).

4. The process of claiming your worth will likely bring up powerful thoughts and feelings. *Aspect Two, Freedom from the Mind* and the section *Working with Pain* in *Aspect Three, Mindfulness*, can help you navigate both. Seek professional support if necessary.

5. Experiment. Look in the mirror – at your whole self, if you can, and not just your first impression of your "looks". Ask yourself, "What do I see? Do I see myself accurately?" As part of overcoming the distortion of the mind, imagine asking a trusted person what they see. If there are ways in which you are inaccurate, enlist the support of someone close to you to help.

6. Consider focusing on self-acceptance. Intrinsic worth means that you will need to accept your imperfections and innate fallibility as being human and not proof of unworthiness. If you

have not already done that acceptance work, it will be hard not to feel unworthy and shameful when your imperfections and your fallibility arise, as they inevitability will. Accepting yourself is to do so entirely, right now, as is. Think of the joy of the imperfect pet or car, or your child. The imperfections are what make them who they are, precious in their uniqueness. Imagine standing at a funeral of someone you love. The best story you can tell, the most endearing, is likely of their human side. Now turn that onto yourself. Be that person at your funeral, celebrating your humanity with love, humor, and dignity.

If self-acceptance is challenging, starting with smaller parts of yourself that you struggle with can be helpful. It is also a good idea to focus on parts of yourself that you have no choice around, such as changes due to aging. Consider this: if you cannot change this imperfection or fallibility, and acceptance brings peace, why would you want to continue to suffer?

Often accepting yourself is tangled up in whether or not others accept you. If relying on others for a sense of acceptance is a part of the river where you get stuck, consider that you may be projecting. Perhaps they accept you and don't judge you at all. Have you asked them? Ultimately, if you are being authentic, in the rare occurrence where you accept yourself, and someone else doesn't, you can decide how much that matters to you and what you want to do about it.

7. Sometimes a belief of unworthiness is linked to an act or choice from the past. If this is true for you, offer yourself forgiveness for the mistakes you have made and those you have hurt. If you have not made yourself available to repair injuries that you have caused, consider doing so, making it an active

versus passive process. *Aspect Seven*, on *Conscious Relationships*, offers a model for healing relational injuries.

8. Set and maintain boundaries as one of the external markers of embodied intrinsic worth. Remember that if you are worthy, then you matter, and if you matter, then what you want and need matters as well. There is more on boundaries in *Aspect Seven, Conscious Relationships*.

## Stories from the field...

Keith wouldn't look at me at first; his eyes focused on the carpet for pretty much all of a session. He came in with his wife, Kara, to do relationship work, and was very quiet in the sessions. When he did speak, he began most of his sentences with, "I don't know." He continued personal work after his start with couples counseling. Over time, Keith slowly engaged more directly with me, making eye contact, and offering a little bit more of himself. Keith's way of retreating and not expressing himself came from a deep sense of worthlessness; things had happened in his childhood that led to a story that he carried into his adult life and into his marriage to Kara. His father was virtually absent for much of his youth, and the little contact Keith had with him always left him wanting more. As a child and continuing through his adult life, his father's absence left a scar of not feeling good enough for the attention and relationship he needed and longed for; those instances led to a core belief that the lack of attention from his dad was a direct reflection of how much Keith mattered. He took it personally and suffered from disappointment and ongoing depression. Sadly, his mind interpreted life events such that his story of being unworthy was confirmed over and over again. It took time, receptivity, and tenacity on his part to overcome this childhood belief. He began to recognize that the belief he held was born out of circumstances, not the truth. He was able to see that the lack of attention and relationship with his dad was about his father, not him. He also had to heal through feeling the emotions involved: sadness, confusion, anger, and ultimately love for the injured part that needed his dad.

Not long ago, his father passed away. In the few years before his dad's passing and particularly in the days leading up to it, Keith had engaged in powerful conversations that illuminated what the truth was. As it turns out, his dad also longed for a relationship with Keith; he just didn't know how to create it. His verbalized remorse contributed significantly to Keith's healing.

Over time, a different Keith has emerged. I can see it as he looks at me, as he speaks with more confidence and directness, and now offers his insight and wisdom to others. It wasn't an overnight process. In knowing I wanted to tell his story, he was surprised I chose him. I did because he represents to me the embodiment of claiming intrinsic worth by doing the hard work of challenging his beliefs and healing his pain.

♦

Note: The following story is one of several I include throughout the book that are written in first person by someone who reflects a particular aspect of wakefulness.

"My whole life, I had heard the words "You are worthy, special, and perfect in your imperfect way." These words always helped me know how much I was loved and I always assumed that I believed it myself. But in my mid-twenties, deep feelings of unworthiness surfaced, and though I conveyed confidence every day and truly loved life itself, I discovered that I disliked much about myself. There was a dissonance between what I knew at a core level (I am worthy) and what I felt (I should be better). I kept telling myself I had worth and deserved to be loved, but I didn't *feel* it. The fact that I couldn't feel it made it even worse because I felt like I was letting my parents down.

As the reality of how I felt came crashing down, I had to start with claiming my worth within myself and not rely on my parents, anyone else, or even my circumstances to assure me. That meant that I had to separate those things I thought made me unworthy and face them on their own, not as evidence that I wasn't enough but that they were parts of my life that needed attention and change. These were issues I had been actively avoiding for years, including not feeling comfortable in my body, facing relationship concerns, and reframing multiple job changes from failure to an exploration for finding my professional path. In meeting my challenges with honesty, love, and hope, I felt stronger; as that strength grew, so did the recognition that my intrinsic worth had been with me all along. Feeling empowered and resilient was what brought me back to truly and unconditionally loving myself. At that point, I knew that no matter what situation life brings forth, I have the strength, love, and courage within myself to conquer anything…because I am worthy and I am enough."

## Longing to Belong

Having navigated what for some is the biggest boulder in the river, intrinsic worth, another obstacle may come into view. That boulder is your sense of belonging. Without an abiding experience of interconnectedness with others, you are trapped in the eddy of trying to bridge your feelings of separation with attempts to connect. But imagine knowing you are already connected so that you don't have to work at it. Imagine further a possibility of feeling that connection whether or not you have a partner right now or a friend to accompany you to a movie. Like with intrinsic worth, you can feel a stronger sense of belonging by defining yourself as part of the whole. But if feeling connected to others is still a challenge, if you never felt like you belonged to your family or had a tribe of your own, this section may help.

As humans, we need a sense of belonging to live fully as our awakened self. The need for connection is a part of our makeup, biologically and psychologically. We are wired to track what's happening with others. Our mind notices, "Do I belong?" and "Am I being included or excluded?" The loneliness that ensues without a strong sense of belonging illustrates the importance of feeling tethered to others in a meaningful way.

Our sense of belonging has roots in the past. Belonging is one of the critical building blocks in childhood. In our early years, it happens in two ways, and both are very important. First, a sense of belonging comes from family. Pause right now and ask yourself whether you felt like you belonged to your family. Even in families where there was love and support, sometimes the sense of belonging was missing. In those cases, sometimes children will adopt a different family, one in which they feel similar to, welcomed, and seen.

For those children who don't have a surrogate family available, thankfully, there is a second source to give a child a sense of belonging: with friends and peers. Social acceptance, feeling like you have a place in the world, is part of the foundation of your sense of self; it builds ego-strength, as described earlier. Unfortunately, sometimes we are not socially accepted. For those who aren't, a belief that "I don't belong" is often coupled with many feelings, including loneliness, anger, and despair. If you were one of those kids who had few to no friends, were rejected because you were different, or worse yet, were bullied, you may carry the scars of not feeling or believing that you belong.

The best scenario for all of us is to receive a sense of belonging from both family and the world outside of our home. Many people, however, get a sense of belonging from only one of these two sources. Some do not get a sense of belonging from either. When this essential human need is not fully met, it often shows up in adult life, appearing as always feeling left out or a vague sense of being on the outside of life looking in.

Like with the belief "I am unworthy", the belief "I don't belong" accompanies you and becomes a filter through which you experience the world and interpret life events; experiences that appear as evidence that reinforces the belief that you don't belong. For example, picture the person desperately wanting to connect, but because they already feel disconnected to others, comes late and leaves early from the yoga class, finding a spot in the back and not making much eye contact. They are doing this because they feel disconnected. Sadly, their behavior reinforces the belief of not belonging. Why? Because people that come late, leave early, and don't make eye contact make connection difficult.

There is a considerable range for people regarding what is enough connectedness and sense of belonging. No one size fits all. What's important is getting enough of a sense of belonging so you travel through life with a feeling and belief of connectedness. Introverts, for example, need less time with others to be connected, and with too much time start to feel disconnected.

For any of us who need solitude from time to time, which is most if not all of us, seeking solitude from a place of connection and as a function of having autonomy is entirely different than seeking isolation from a place of disconnection or avoidance. Isolation is hallmarked by a sense of shutting down and retreating from others and life, often with fear, hurt, or distrust. Solitude, on the other hand, is the positive, and more temporary, connective movement toward oneself. With solitude, there is no fear or distrust. The sense of being connected to others accompanies us as we seek solitude.

Restoring a sense of belonging is similar to recognizing your intrinsic worth. It is *not* about getting more friends or joining more groups. Initially, it's an inside job. Gaining a sense of belonging is about changing the core belief about belonging. You belong, intrinsically, whether you know it or not and whether your circumstances or upbringing gave you that message or not. Belonging is not due to a result of fitting in but because you exist. I am speaking to a deep sense of this, not to the more superficial feeling of being part of a community based on interest, age, or politics, for example. Intrinsic belonging means that you know yourself as an integral part of the human race and to all living things. Whatever way you define the whole, you are already part of it.

## Practice

1. Reflect upon experiences where you feel you didn't belong, or where you felt left out. Were your experiences an interpretation of what was happening or a projection onto others? Did you stay disengaged because you didn't feel connected, and therefore experienced a self-fulfilling prophecy when your projections became real-life experiences? Consider for this practice idea and the one to follow journaling your reflections. Then take notice of any shift in your sense of belonging.

2. Reflect also upon your family of origin and your upbringing in your childhood. Did you get the message from your family and the outside world that you belonged? If you did not or felt you were different in any way, this message may not have been communicated to you. Humans tend to flock to what is familiar and reject what is not. Did something like that happen to you? If so, you may have internalized a message based on circumstance rather than truth.

3.  Challenge your beliefs around belonging and work through any emotions that might come up. *Aspect Two, Freedom from the Mind* and the section *Working with Pain* in *Aspect Three, Mindfulness*, can help you do both. Seek professional support if necessary.

4.  Every day, identify someone who initially feels different than you and find at least three things that you have in common.

## *Stories from the field . . .*

Lauren came from a large family, the youngest of five girls. As an adult, just like in her childhood, she had a specific role in her family. That role kept a deeply held fear that she didn't belong at bay. Unfortunately, staying in a particular role as a daughter and sister kept her trapped in ways of being that no longer served her. Doing so also did not always reflect her authentic self. It has taken courage to do the personal work of facing her fear as she invited her roles in life to change. Without a role to protect her, she has had to ask herself whether or not she belongs, without having to do or be anything. She has found that belonging, at its core, is not about what she does or the contribution she makes. It is, like intrinsic worth, about being, not doing. Lauren belongs because she is innately part of the whole. Her imperfect, human, and big-hearted self belongs, without any agenda of what she has to do in life. This level of freedom is new and exciting. As she engages with her family as her awakened self, void of having to be in a role to ensure her place, not only has it changed her life, but it also offers something different and better to those she loves.

# *Self-Love*

Intrinsic worth, a sense of belonging, knowing yourself as someone extraordinary – perhaps you are already swimming in a beautiful pool of self-love. But for some, declaring that we love ourselves is complicated; it feels challenging and uncomfortable because the words speak of selfishness and narcissism or seem like part of living in the ego. Self-love can feel impossible because of the long list of grievances we carry against ourselves. It can also feel disingenuous; we're supposed to love ourselves, but the truth is we don't.

How about you? Are you uncomfortable with the idea of loving yourself? Maybe the words bring you a warm and positive feeling. If so, you are fortunate. Without it, you are out of the flow of the current and stuck in yet another eddy that can hold you back from being in the flow of wakefulness. I encourage you to be curious about any resistance you have to self-love, as there is an opportunity for insight and healing in exploring what stands in the way.

Since self-love is the hallmark of living as your awakened self, it is essential for you to know where you are. So let's start with getting a sense for how self-loving you are right now. One way to know where you are is to see how often you find yourself in self-loathing, the opposite of self-love. Much of self-loathing is based on old beliefs such as "I am not lovable" or experiences of not feeling loved. Any experience of not being loved, followed by a belief that you are not lovable gives context to why you might struggle with loving yourself. A radical new perspective can be this: perhaps your experience about being unloved wasn't about you at all. Maybe, instead, it was about the capacity of the other person to love. This new understanding can be immense in terms of helping undo the belief "I am unlovable." The reality is that for some of us, one or both of our parents were limited in their capacity to love. When we can recognize this, we can offer ourselves the truth: "I am lovable."

Intrinsic worth, or the lack of it, also plays a role. If you have believed yourself to be unworthy, it would have been nearly impossible to love yourself fully. If you have not accepted yourself, including your fallibility, then your mistakes and imperfections become fuel for the fire of self-loathing.

If you need more motivation to love yourself, consider how much time and space are eaten up by *not* loving yourself. A harsh inner critic ready to pounce in a nanosecond keeps you preoccupied with negative thoughts toward yourself. In addition to being distracted, you probably feel depressed and anxious. Then your depression and anxiety takes up more space and distracts you further.

Not loving yourself has a significant impact on others as well. As you contend with the relentless self-absorption that occurs with self-evaluation and self-criticism, you aren't present and available to others. When you don't love yourself, you fail others in this way. This dramatic realization can lead to the awareness that loving yourself is the highest form of loving others. No longer lost in the trance of self-absorption, you can offer others your full and relaxed presence.

Finally, if you are still having trouble with the idea of self-love, see if your expanded definition of who you are makes it easier. Self-loathing is about living from the old paradigm of who you thought you were. Self-love is about living as your awakened self as part of the gorgeous, majestic, and mysterious whole. Below are some other ideas that may help.

*Practice*

1.  One of the simplest ways to embody self-love is to start being kinder to yourself. Something internally changes once you start doing that. It's like a part of you notices what you are doing and starts to orient in that direction, as if this is a new North Star to follow.

2.  Pay attention to your self-talk and begin to work with it. Picture what it would be like to put your self-talk on a loudspeaker. Or imagine speaking to another the way you would speak to yourself. A self-loving inner dialogue is a stark contrast to a harsh inner critic, what many of us have lived with for years. While you can't always change the negative, critical, and judgmental thoughts from happening, you can begin to talk to yourself in a compassionate, patient, and kind way. As you try it, see how it feels. If it feels uncomfortable, try to see that your discomfort is usually a sign that you are breaking through something. If it feels nearly impossible to offer kind words to yourself, pretend you are speaking to yourself as a child or a dear friend.

3.  In addition to focusing on your self-talk, self-expression in your outer world is another great place to practice loving yourself. Self-expression means you value your voice. Imagine what it would be like to have something to say that is wanting to burst forth, but having a thick steel plate in your throat, unmoving and solid. That plate represents you withholding from yourself something essential: self-expression. The words and ideas underneath can't come up and out, and everything inside becomes dense and blocked. But when you love yourself, you give, you don't withhold. So go back to the steel plate. Now imagine it transforming into crystal clear water

drops, and your voice, like a fountain, emerging as a waterfall, beautiful and strong. That's the way it can feel.

In practicing self-expression, do so consciously. From the perspective of your awakened self, remember it is how you express yourself, not only if you express yourself. Raging at someone because you feel angry is not your most wakeful self-expression. Emotionally regulated, clear, and honest communication is a reflection of the kind of self-expression of which I'm speaking. Speaking your truth means expressing yourself not from your ego, or in a way that dominates, or seeks approval of others. Instead, it is self-expression that comes out of self-love and offers a sense of connection and safety for the other. For some, this will mean expressing yourself more or differently than ever before. Aspect Seven, Conscious Relationships offers ideas and practices that help with emotional regulation as part of conscious communication.

4.  Sometimes how self-loving you are shows up as your level of self-nurturing. Just like self-expression, self-love does not withhold; it offers. So when you don't get enough sleep, or don't ever take a day off to relax, you are not nurturing yourself; you are not practicing self-love. Nurturing yourself, then, becomes a place to strengthen your self-love. Sometimes it can be as easy as using the restroom when you need it but could also be as new and different as taking a trip by yourself.

### Stories from the field . . .

Katrina is a beautiful, healthy yoga teacher. She also finds great meaning in her work at a nonprofit. Her life looks ideal to everyone around her. She takes care of herself on the outside. But inside is a different story. Katrina lives every day with a harsh inner critical voice that tells her she is unlovable and will never overcome a past that haunts her, among other inaccurate and judgmental messages. The result was that in many areas of her life she had to be perfect to compensate. So she tried to be perfect, which left her highly anxious and consistently distracted since her goal of perfectionism was both unattainable and unsustainable. In working with the idea of self-love, Katrina couldn't start with deciding to love herself. She's had to take it one step at a time. She is beginning to be kind as she speaks to herself. She is learning to challenge her old and inaccurate beliefs about herself, as well as be realistic in what she aims to achieve. Her self-care practices are changing too. Instead of intense workouts due to fear and obligation, she listens to her body and has become gentler with herself. Her process hasn't been quick, but each step brings her closer to self-love.

## Your Ego: Friend or Foe?

So far, your ego has been described as both friend and foe. A friend that protects you and a foe that interferes with living as your awakened self. If you can establish a friendly relationship with your ego, it will go a long way in living as your awakened self. I'll start with a quick reminder of the importance of your ego before I offer some ideas for working with, and not against it.

Bottom line, without an ego, I would not be writing this book, you likely would not be reading it, and much of our life success would not be ours to enjoy; this is because of the essential role the ego plays in our development.

As mentioned before, ego development gives you ego-strength, and early in life, a sense of who you are. Without an identity at that point in your life, you are lost. Beyond forming an initial identity, there is no doubt your ego-strength has also gotten you far in life as it served to motivate you, giving you the drive to survive and an interest in achieving your goals. And also remember the protection it offers. That safeguard is enormous, especially when you are young. Whether it helped you to disassociate when emotions were too intense or created other ways for you to defend against pain, you wouldn't have survived your inner pain without your ego.

I have found it helpful to keep a few things in mind when working with the ego. First, your ego hates deprivation. When you feel deprived, the volume of desire usually turns up, along with panic. Think about all of those times you tried to quit something in an extreme way. Did you find yourself wanting what you wanted even more? Practicing generosity toward yourself without being indulgent can prevent your ego from rearing up because it feels deprived. Secondly, the ego likes to look good. Working with this idea is useful. Imagine just redefining what "looking good" means. If you define it as being humble, making mistakes, having wrinkles, and being proud of your imperfections, your ego gets to "look good" by you living as your awakened, authentic self.

Finally, as with all parts of human existence, it is unwise to deny or judge this part of you. Though some on a spiritual path believe there is no place for ego, I have seen that position to have the opposite effect: an ego that shows up when you least expect or want it to appear. I invite you to hold it in your heart as a dear friend and companion who has contributed much along the way.

## Practice

1. Reflect upon how your ego has served you. Imagine offering recognition and acknowledgment to your ego for what it has given you. You can even start a dialogue with your ego. Ask it what it needs. Consider writing all of this down.

2. Be accountable. Reflect upon and journal about when and how your ego shows up. Pay attention to how it interferes with living wakefully, such as in a relationship, in the form of defensiveness, rationalization, retaliation or punishment, competition, or in cravings that result in compulsivity. You can see your ego controlling you when you find yourself being strategic, such as going for the best seat in the house, managing information to your benefit, or shielding a part of you from others.

Your accountability directly correlates to how much your ego is in charge. The more responsibility you take, which is humbling, the greater your ability to keep your ego in check. Make sure, as you are holding yourself more accountable, that you always affirm your intrinsic worth. Your worth is never on the line, no matter what you have done or said; knowing this will allow for the greatest amount of accountability.

### *Stories from the field . . .*

This story is about someone who exhibits being in the world without a lot of ego. When I met Roxanne, she was already there. In working with her, I discovered many things that made it possible. She has a positive regard for herself without a sense of superiority. She listens well, doesn't make assumptions, and is curious. She is kind to herself without being indulgent. Roxanne is able to hear things easily and be honest with herself. If there is a part she has played in something that has happened, she readily takes responsibility. Roxanne has had her difficulties, childhood and otherwise. But she lives in the world without the sense of armoring or need to impress that reflects living from one's ego. I have worked with her for years and continue to be inspired by her receptivity and open posture to others and to life. Roxanne is not a person who goes around saying, "I have transcended my ego!" And that is the very point.

# Aspect Two
## Freedom from your Mind

Traveling downriver to the relationship you have with your mind is where we go next. Distinguishing between your mind as it serves you and the thoughts that disturb you is essential as we explore this *Aspect of Wakefulness*. Survival, functionality, organization, creativity, invention, insight, and many other capacities are the gifts of your mind. These gifts are a powerful part of your existence. Freedom from your mind is freedom from the kind of redundant thinking that generates anxiety as well as stress and at times does not see a situation or others clearly.

Much human suffering can be directly linked to thoughts that are believed, stories that are woven, and projections that are trusted. The idea that there is another alternative, that there is the possibility of *not* believing a thought or a story, can be transformative. It's like getting out from under the cloudiness of the mind into an expanse of clear blue sky.

You may have already realized that your thinking is not usually where you find your most profound happiness; some would say it never is. But take a test. When have you felt the happiest and well, mentally and physically? What were you doing? What were you thinking or were you thinking at all? What were you feeling? Did you have a sense of being in the present moment? An active and dominant mind often results in less inner peace, less relaxation, and less contentment. Most of us feel our most alive and at greatest ease when we have freedom from a mind that never ceases.

Breaking away from a part of you that you are used to, that perhaps feels comfortable, and has served you, can be hard. If this is true for you, your loyalty to your mind is not a bad thing. Your commitment is good and endearing. But your devotion to what is familiar and feels comfortable is a problem when your mind keeps you from living as your awakened self.

In exploring this *Aspect of Wakefulness* in your inner world, it might seem like I am encouraging you to reject your mind. But emancipation from your mind is not the rejection of your mind. Freedom from the mind is similar to you leaving home, emancipating yourself from what you had known, and then returning to your family as an adult. You take a step back from a part of you that is dominating your experience to become independent. You return, able to embrace your mind having put it in its honored but limited place. Emancipating from your mind is, of course, easier said than done.

To help in getting motivated to do this emancipation work, let's start with some of the outcomes of a mind run amuck. One of the most important of those outcomes is distortion; a shift away from what is real and true. Your mind isn't always seeing things accurately. I'll bet you've had many experiences of feeling so confident in a perception, only to find it to be completely different than you thought. Distortion of reality in the confines of your mind is like going to an amusement park and standing in front of one of those silly mirrors. The reflection is you but distorted. There are elements that you recognize, but a lot more that is false, and perhaps even bizarre.

Secondly, emotions can be triggered by thoughts, which is different than feelings generated from direct experience. If you have had a pet die, for example, you probably felt sad because of real loss, not sad because you thought your pet might die; this is what I mean by direct experience. You had a direct experience of loss, not a perceived experience of loss. Emotions themselves are never the problem, but a stressful emotion generated by inaccurate thoughts is a problem.

To get a better idea of how a thought and belief can generate feelings, imagine believing that you are unlikable. A belief like this produces lots of emotions. I am sure you can imagine some. But if the belief couples with an event, such as when someone cancels doing something with you, the feelings are ten times worse. Instead of just feeling disappointed because you were looking forward to getting together (a feeling based on direct experience), you feel much worse because you might interpret being unlikeable as the cause of the cancelation. The reality is that sometimes people cancel lunch. They need to do something different. They change their mind, like you. Bottom line: your mind is always trying to connect dots, even when they aren't meant to be connected.

Let's go even further with an example that is far too common: a belief that shows up as a thought, over and over again. These are the beliefs you have that are the most ingrained and probably have roots in the past in the form of messages you received. People and the circumstances of your life communicate different things to you; some are positive; some are negative. When you take those ideas all the way inside of you, they become yours. They live with you like ghosts that continually haunt you. When you look more closely, maybe they go away. But if a thought comes back to haunt you, you can know the reoccurring belief as one that runs deep.

Let's consider messages about you as a person. What if someone or something along the way gave you the message that you were worthless, unlovable, or unattractive? Believing the words, "I am worthless, unlovable, or unattractive" causes that thought to cycle through your mind, typically with depression, anxiety, and despair that follow

As if this is not enough, something else often starts to happen. In believing you are worthless, unlovable, or unattractive, many decisions and choices follow. Though some choices are a great idea, such as being kinder to those around you because you want them to like you, many are not, such as retreating from the world or being a perfectionist to compensate around a sense of inadequacy. Even more concerning are choices that are a form of self-harm, meaning that you punish yourself as a result of believing a thought.

Bottom line, when you believe something big, then big feelings follow, and potentially, many choices as well. Lost in a trance of illusion, you are no longer living as your awakened self. As I described earlier in exploring intrinsic worth and belonging, your beliefs serve as a filter by which you experience the world.

And remember the clincher: your beliefs about the world, yourself, others, and many other parts of life, which live in you as thoughts, look for confirmation; this is part of how they stick around and haunt you. Each of your beliefs, whether it brings you joy or pain, is looking for evidence that affirms it. Sometimes the evidence is real, but often it is not. You will tend to ignore any evidence that does not match your inner beliefs because it is different than what feels true inside. You will also tend to notice most readily evidence that confirms what feels true; this is how misinterpretation happens, often unbeknownst to you. You interpret a situation based on how it fits into your belief system and world view.

A common example is around compliments. Have you been the person or known someone who can't seem to take a compliment? A compliment is rejected when what is offered doesn't match what is felt to be true internally. Sadly, this is when the phrase, "He/she can't take a compliment" is actually true; he/she *can't*! The compliment itself might be the very thing that person yearns to hear and believe. If you believe yourself to be unlovable or unworthy, the compliment, "You are an amazing person" would be the medicine you need to heal. If you could take it in, there would be such restoration. Unfortunately, if what is offered doesn't sync up with your inner scaffolding, it rolls off like water on a duck.

Finally, let's bring this full circle and consider how this part of you affects another part of you: your body. Your body is a finely tuned instrument, susceptible to mental distress, and is impacted by disturbing thoughts. When your highly sensitive nervous system gets a message from your brain that is stressful, it goes into a stress response. If that message is based on untrue thoughts, your body does not know this. It reacts in natural ways as a means of protection and self-preservation. That capacity itself, to respond in times of danger, is amazing and welcomed. But your nervous system becoming agitated and your well-being compromised due to believing an untrue thought or story is an unnecessary form of physical suffering.

An image that can help you see how much you are at the mercy of your thoughts is to see your mind having an imagination party in the form of a movie. Too often, the show is a terrible story with disturbing images, and the party is not fun at all. Without freedom from your mind, you are forced, in a way, to sit down and watch the movie that your mind just created. If what your mind crafted is a horror movie, you feel horrible. If the movie is about a future that looks bleak or a past you cannot recover from, it would be easy to feel hopelessness and shame. You create your suffering as you endure this movie, agonize over its impact, and find yourself stuck in a theatre you cannot escape. Freedom from your mind offers you an escape exit.

Imagine how wonderful it would be if you had a way to ensure that untrue thoughts weren't allowed inside, creating a horror movie, tweaking your nervous system, or generating stressful emotions.

There are a couple of ways I have seen this work. The first is to learn to let thoughts float by as you refuse to engage them. Your inner witness is a great help here because if you stay connected to it, thoughts pass more easily and quickly. You can also try redirecting your attention onto something else. Anything else can work, but a good refocus for your attention can be your breath or substituting something good or beautiful. For example, imagine you were standing in a forest, with your mind going down a rabbit hole. Redirecting your thoughts, you whistle, and then point to the beautiful sunset. Your mind, then, has something different, something better on which to focus.

A second approach to gain freedom from your mind is to develop your capacity to see what is true and what is not. Back on the river, think of this ability to discern truth from fiction as the current underneath you, keeping you on track and not washed up on the bank of illusion.

Let's start with the first idea: increasing your ability to ignore your thoughts and redirect your attention. Meditation is a fantastic way to help you do so.

## Meditation

An active mind, a quiet mind; it makes no difference when you can maintain a different vantage point and don't get caught up in its comings and goings. Meditation offers that different vantage point. Learning how to direct your attention rather than following every thought, regardless of where it leads, can be a huge relief. Picture yourself sitting on a mountain, able to watch the storm of your thoughts below. Perhaps you gaze at that storm with love and without resistance or judgment. You are not in it, just aware of it. The mountain seat offers quiet warmth and a great view. You are immune from the lightning strikes and raindrops below. You can choose to pay attention to the storm or close your eyes, breathe deeply, and enjoy the sun on your shoulders. You get to decide. It's blustering, but you recognize that it will pass, as all storms do.

Your ability to watch the squall is because of your previous work of strengthening your inner witness.

Sitting on the mountaintop, relaxed, is in contrast to when your mind is in control. Those are the times that you head right down the mountain into the eye of the storm. You get wet and turned around, swallowed up in the storm until it passes. And remember that when you get caught in the storm of your thoughts, your body does too, responding by feeling agitated, having shortness of breath or tightness in your chest, and sometimes even experiencing nausea in your belly. The impact of staying out of the storm, through meditation, creates the opposite reaction in your body: relaxation.

So, relaxed and calm on a mountain seat under a clear, blue sky with the warm sun on your shoulders – or – wet, cold, and lost in the storm of your thinking as your body tightens and contracts. What do you choose? I'm guessing that freedom from the storm of your mind sounds a lot more appealing.

Meditation is about experiencing that calm, serene, quiet place in your inner world. One of the most powerful ideas I can offer is that the calm space inside already exists. Really take this in. In meditation, you are not searching for inner peace. There is nothing to acquire. Instead, your inner peace is patiently waiting for you to discover it, tucked within. Internalizing this idea can be huge in helping you not stress about making something happen when you meditate. It is your best starting place.

Before I understood this premise, the strain of trying so hard to be calm while I sat still was quite nerve racking! Since then, by knowing that serenity already lives inside of me, I can drop much more quickly into the experience of it. I encourage you to spend time with this idea before you even start to explore a meditation practice of your own. Let it roll around inside of you as a possibility, so that when you do begin meditating, you have the gift of knowing that your only job is to relax into what is already there.

There are many approaches to the practice of meditation. I recommend keeping it simple and doable so that it can be part of a full life. In my life, I have meditated for many hours and days at a time. Those experiences deepened my practice considerably and offered a profound sense of expansiveness, peace, and love. But those uninterrupted hours and days are not always available in my life. Thankfully, I have discovered that a daily practice offers some of what can be experienced in a meditation retreat, especially when you have consistency.

Most mornings I sit, with eyes open or closed, with a warm cup of coffee before my day begins. For 3-5 minutes I stop, pause, and enjoy the sensory experience of the warmth on my hands and the experience of my body waking up. Usually, I feel an immediate connection to the peace that lives within me. I try to feel my breath throughout my body such that it feels like I am living in my skin, rather than my head. I also stay anchored in the present moment, not allowing the past or future to be my focus. I let the current moment take up all of my attention. I finish with the idea of turning toward myself, without agenda, taking a kind and curious stance. When emotions and body sensations show up, I tune in. And if my mind wants to get active in planning or fixing, I keep inviting it to rest.

This daily practice is a sweet way to start my day, and because it is easy, I do it. I travel through the rest of my day feeling in touch with the calmness within me, with greater freedom from my mind, and more connected to my body and myself. As you can imagine, this is much better than starting my day with an emphasis on what I have to do and where I need to be, tired before I even begin, with an unrelenting stream of thoughts that fill my head and drive my body.

I recommend several other ways to begin bringing meditation into your life, both here and in the practice section. First, and most importantly, see if you can find a few moments each day to be still, whether you use my 3-5 minute ritual or develop one of your own. It doesn't have to be complicated. It can happen in the morning or at night. Perhaps your practice happens with a cup of tea or even in the shower if you have a hard time finding a way to be uninterrupted for a short time. Maybe, instead, it is best to have a ritual at the end of your day, finding a moment or two to stop and be in stillness. The point is to start with something – anything – and to make it fit easily into your life. The hope is that you like it and that you find yourself engaging in the ritual regularly and for extended amounts of time.

Beyond a very short daily practice, consider starting a simple meditation practice for 10-15 minutes, if not every day, several times a week. If this appeals to you, try to create a space where you will be undisturbed. It can be helpful to have candlelight and a soft, comfortable place to sit. By making a physical space for meditation, it encourages the space to open up in your inner world. That said, a beautiful meditation room will only agitate you if you don't use it.

Below is a step-by-step process you can use to begin:

- Find a quiet place.

- As you settle in, make sure you are physically comfortable, perhaps with cushions, a blanket, etc.

- With your eyes closed, put your attention on your breathing, deepening your breath over the first few minutes. As you do this, imagine your breath reaching the tips of your toes and rising to the top of your head.

- If you can, stay with your breath, and as thoughts arise, watch them pass. If you find yourself following your thoughts, redirect your focus back onto your breath. With your breath as a focal point, and as you acknowledge but refuse to engage your thoughts, eventually your mind quiets. Dramatic thoughts, benign thoughts, and everything in between start to float by. The real trick here is to be patient with a mind that might need time to settle down.

- If focusing only on your breath is difficult, you can also work with a mantra. A mantra is a simple word or phrase such as "I am loved", "peace", or even the word "rest". Keep gently repeating the word or phrase.

While the process is simple and *gets* easier, it isn't usually comfortable at first. The immediate and demanding flood of thoughts that occur when you get started is challenging for many beginning meditators. If this happens to you, rather than fighting your mind, accept that, for today, it is active.

I like to suggest images to work with. When your mind is busy and trying to distract you, think of it as a child who is jumping up and down demanding attention. Arguing or becoming angry with that child only stokes the fire. And while what that child is saying may be something compelling, with love, you remain vigilant in returning again and again to your breath or mantra. If you have been enjoying the imagery of being the river traveling toward the ocean, picture each thought as a cloud floating over you. The cloud may be beautiful or a dark rain cloud; regardless, it is temporary. It passes, and your job is to let it go by. Finally, you can picture thoughts as a bunch of little old ladies or men chatting away in the back of the room. Smile at those chatting and decide not to eavesdrop. Each and all of these images, or any that come to you on your own, are a wonderful way to work with, and not against, your mind. Ultimately, taking a relaxed and loving stance helps an active mind to settle. I can tell you from my experience and that of many others, if you fight your busy mind, it will create a power struggle, which ironically will continue to activate your thinking. When you accept rather than resist your active mind, however, the opposite happens.

As we shift to challenging your thoughts, know that the more you practice meditation, the more your attention, like a rudder of a boat, knows where to turn. You are creating deep neural pathways as you repeat the process of meditation, and gaining freedom from your mind in the process. When caught in the eddy of a swirling mind, meditation offers a way back to the current of your awakened life.

## Challenging Your Thoughts

If your thoughts are on a merry-go-round, meditation allows you to step off. But what about those thoughts that keep you stuck on the merry-go-round? Or back to our river metaphor, what about an eddy that, like real-life eddies, actually causes deeper stuff to come to the surface. No matter how much you try to ignore your thoughts, and no matter how many deep breaths you take, you can't get back to the current. Those are the thoughts you need to challenge.

A great starting place is to dive into the waters of how the thought happened in the first place. That alone can be a way to defy the legitimacy of any given belief. If a thought is disturbing to you, ask the question, "How did it get here?" Consider that the particular thought, and for that matter, any thought you have, may have come from outside of you; something you heard said or was said directly to you. You then made it your own. When you can picture a disturbing thought coming from *outside* before it got *inside* your head, you are getting closer to being free from its power. Taking a step further, remember that you were not in control of much of what has happened to you, especially at a young age. Those two things: how easily it is to internalize something from the outside and the fact that you were not in control of what messages you received, may help you challenge the overall premise of any given thought.

Let me give you an example. If your teacher in second grade said that you did something stupid or, worse yet, called you stupid, the circulating thought of "I am stupid" was something you heard from someone else, and was not originally yours. Children take things literally and personally as they develop their sense of self. In this case, the teacher may not have meant that you were stupid; instead, they may have been speaking of a behavior. Nonetheless, it may have been taken in as a literally true statement. Even if the teacher did mean to say that you were stupid (a frightening prospect), that would still only be their perspective and most likely about their own sense of inadequacy. Bottom line, any thought in your head may be a reflection of someone else's view or opinion. Knowing this leaves you in a strong position to reject the idea based on its source.

Given the premise that your thoughts arise from your experience and influences outside of your control, who then is responsible for your thoughts? Take in this question. What if it is not you? That possibility is quite extraordinary since most of us have spent years being driven by our thinking, and feeling shamed by its content. Your freedom lies in knowing that your thoughts are not you, and are not yours. However they came to exist in your mind, in a way, matters not. What matters is what you do with them.

As you begin to see that you are not to blame for what you think, it becomes much easier to let go of any given thought or belief purely because you didn't create it. With this awareness, you can reject a thought or belief. You can genuinely embody these wise words: "Don't own your thoughts and don't let them own you." Even intense thoughts – like suicide, adultery, homicide, and other thoughts that freak most of us out – are less of a problem from this perspective. Those thoughts are just darker and more intense clouds that ultimately still float by.

Being free from assuming responsibility for your thoughts can go a far distance in challenging your thoughts. What can be additionally helpful is to let yourself become bored and disinterested with repetitive thoughts. Really, how entertaining is it to watch the merry-go-round of thought loop over and over again? Pretty unappealing over time, as nothing changes, and eventually, the color fades. Perhaps you can even imagine being entertained by a mind that keeps trying to get you riled up. It's like sitting in the bleachers watching as your mind works to keep your attention by doing the same tricks over and over again.

Finally, let's delve into thoughts or beliefs that are powerful enough that they feel like the merry-go-round itself; thoughts that are so big and heavy that they seem unaffected by any attempts to become free. You've tried not taking responsibility for the thought, as well as encouraged yourself to become bored and disinterested with the repetition. But somehow you still find yourself caught in the eddy of that belief. If so, you may have to challenge it directly.

To begin, imagine inviting the thought or belief to sit down with you on an inner bench and have a conversation. Picture yourself asking the question, "Are you true?" Then, explore what makes that thought feel true to you. In your curiosity, start asking what evidence exists to support that thought, and is there any other evidence to the contrary? Remember that a thought or belief *feeling* true does not mean that it *is*.

Looking actively for evidence on both sides gives you neutrality, and in your neutrality, you get a taste of freedom from that thought. Often, you will discover that the thought is not entirely true, or at least not accurate all of the time. You might even find that it only *might* be true, but you don't have enough information to know for sure. And sometimes, something powerful happens with your inquiry. You realize that the thought, belief, or story is false; there is no truth in it at all. And because of this, the thought no longer has power over you. From that place of recognition, all you need to do when that thought returns from time to time is to remind yourself what you've already discovered to be true.

To make this your own, start with a disturbing or stressful thought, such as the common one of "I have to get to sleep now or tomorrow will be awful." When a thought like that is dominating your attention, in this case, literally keeping you up when you want to sleep, it's a great opportunity to challenge it. Pull out your inner bench and invite the thought to sit down. Inquire within yourself, "Is it really true that my day will be terrible if I am sleep deprived?" You can know that there is no absolute truth in it, since it is a thought about the future, and the future hasn't arrived. And in terms of this particular thought, you can ask yourself, "Are there not as many times where I didn't suffer from feeling sleep deprived as there are of times when I did?" And even if you do suffer, meaning you are extra tired the next day, isn't it possible that you can handle it, and handle it well? Think about the days you make it through, happily surprised by your energy despite your lack of sleep.

Freedom from your mind means that you never assume a thought or belief to be true, and offers significant relief from the impact of distressing thoughts. This realization is the "pause" that gets you out of the eddy. Being stuck in the eddy compromises your happiness, so when you are then able to challenge a particular thought directly, it is transformative. Beliefs such as "I am not enough" or "I don't belong", where the mind has for years been busy looking for verification, no longer live in you as fact. In the process of becoming free from your thoughts, a deep sense of inner peace and self-love emerges. Don't be surprised if you also feel sad as you grieve on behalf of your unnecessary suffering due to your thoughts. Your grief marks self-love, and the invitation is to allow yourself to feel it.

Just as your happiness is well served by challenging your thoughts, and so are your relationships. If you have a belief or thought about someone, which is a projection, and react to it as if it is true, there can be tremendous damage. Making assumptions by believing your unconfirmed thoughts creates injury and distance.

By challenging your thoughts and beliefs, you offer others the same neutrality and curiosity that you experience for yourself. From there, you can ask others what is true as a way of checking out your projections. In doing so, you get to feel more open, less reactive, and more present in your relationships and they get to feel better too. The people in your life will love not having to wade through the stories that you have made up about them. Feeling safe and being understood are the precursors for real intimacy and vulnerability. So often a lack of intimacy and depth is about the blackberry vines of illusion and misunderstanding getting in the way.

If you can, picture yourself standing in front of all the people you know as they make a circle around you. Make sure to include the ones you love and let them stand closest to you. Your commitment to challenge untrue thoughts and beliefs is a form of love you offer. Your experience *of* them is your direct experience *with* them, which means that when you take your thoughts and projections to task, it is like putting a warm shawl around each in the circle.

## *Practice*

1. Start a simple, consistent practice of meditation and being still. Use the one I offered or look for one via podcasts, books, or available through a meditation community. A couple I like are:

   www.meditationoasis.com
   www.themeditationpodcast.com

2. Be prepared for a flood of thought and distraction, especially initially. Stay with the practice patiently, and know you will get better at returning the rudder of your attention to the stillness within you, even if you are restless and uncomfortable at the start.

3. Attend a meditation retreat, as doing so will exponentially help you gain emancipation from your mind. Many retreat centers offer silent weekends that don't include a teacher or a commitment to a specific form of meditation.

4. When beginning to challenge your thoughts, assume nothing in terms of the content of your thoughts and beliefs. Take a neutral stance in that you don't necessarily believe any thought. It is merely a sentence that floats away.

5. Inquire whether a thought is true, and consider what information you have and don't have.

6. Especially for those thoughts that are disturbing and stressful, be aware of the tendency of your mind to find evidence to affirm them (confirmation bias), even after you have determined that they are not true.

7. Check out additional resources that can help you to challenge your thoughts. Byron Katie is an amazing teacher and resource and can be found at www.thework.com.

## *Stories from the field . . .*

Teagan is smart. She has a fulfilling professional life, is happily married, and the parent of a healthy, active daughter. She also has a strong and loving support system. But Teagan was caught in the eddy of deeply disturbing thoughts around her lovability, worth, and trusting others. She knew in her head she was worthy, that people loved her and could be trusted in their love, but somewhere inside, another part of her believed differently; her thoughts created great pain as she continued to see evidence of their truth. When she woke up to the falsehood of her projections and her inaccuracy in seeing herself as unlovable and others as eventually going to leave her, something broke inside of her – in a good way. She became free of the trance of her illusions and the emotional suffering they caused. I can see it in her eyes, her body, and her disposition. Increasingly, she is not at the mercy of her undisciplined mind. Teagan now enjoys greater peace and calm, both within herself and in relationships she can trust.

# Aspect Three
## Practicing Mindfulness

*Mindfulness: Present awareness with acceptance; an ability to stay or return our focus to the present moment.*

Following the current of the river, deeply connected in relationship to yourself, and having traversed the rapids of your mind, we round the bend and discover the beautiful, clear swimming hole of mindfulness; a place to bask, play, and enjoy what is here and now, not preoccupied with the rapids you just came over or what lies ahead. It is to feel Emma's quote fully: "The beautifulness is everywhere!"

Time seems to pass by ever more quickly these days. Pause and ask yourself how aware you are of each moment; are you able to stay in each moment or do you continuously anticipate the next or hold on to the last? Mindfulness is "the ability to be fully present in the moment with acceptance" and is a foundational part of living as your awakened self; this means being present, and not distracted, in a moment-by-moment kind of way. In terms of the great moments, you are probably excited to experience them more fully. But true mindfulness is your ability to be present with *all* of the moments, not just the easy or pleasant ones.

One of the best parts of practicing mindfulness is a respite from a mind continually distracting you from what is happening right now. While distraction may have been an important coping strategy to avoid difficult moments in the past, there is a price to be paid. Distraction takes energy, and you miss out on so much.

Mindfulness, on the other hand, opens up a whole new world. In practicing mindfulness, there is a growing realization that each present moment is one that you can not only "handle", but living in it is the most compelling place to be.

I invite you to test the waters of your capacity to stay in each moment as it unfolds. It will mean being disciplined with a mind that wants to wander into the past or future. It also means you are willing to be with *whatever* is happening in the moment, even when it is uncomfortable, painful, or boring. The opportunity here is that you stop believing you need to get out of any moment. You discover directly what each moment offers, just as you would be discovering what the swimming hole is like by swimming in it.

As you practice mindfulness, one of two things will happen. Either you discover what you've been missing, such as noticing the colors of the bird you just heard chirping, or you will feel some kind of discomfort. As you enjoy the beauty of seeing the bird's colors, along with anything else you've been missing, you might be asking yourself what took you so long to be mindful. But your discomfort provides the answer, since you, like others, may tend to veer away from what is difficult and focus on what feels safe. Practicing mindfulness and being uncomfortable is very different than always feeling blissful and calm.

Maybe it is the overwhelming flood of feelings, or an active mind that won't stop, or even a new level of intimacy with another that tempts you to retreat from the moment. If you've been busy distracting yourself and don't know how to contend with each of those experiences, then being mindful is a stretch. Therefore, it is important to be compassionate and patient as you encourage yourself to stay present through what shows up. When and if it seems to be too much, you can always distract yourself as you have done in the past, though hopefully only temporarily.

One of the great things about testing these waters is that you get to uncover a set of inner resources that you might never have known you had. Imagine that within you exists an ability to deal with waters that are cold and places in the river where there are rocks to navigate. Knowing and trusting your capacity to be with your direct experience is like trusting the current to keep you flowing around the rocks and toward the ocean. The capacity is there, whether or not you have felt or trusted it before. And like all capacities, it grows as you use it.

Let's dive further into what I mean by the inner resources needed to feel equipped to navigate the waters of mindfulness. One of them is your inner witness, which we explored in *Aspect One, Befriending You*. Accessing your inner witness is a way to welcome your moment-by-moment experience from a place of calm, relaxed observance. It goes something like this: "I don't like the depression I am feeling right now, but I can observe it from a place of calm, rather than resist what is uncomfortable." Or, "I can notice that I am bored without rushing to fill the space."

Your ability to befriend what is real and true, rather than fight it, is an additional inner capability you have. Doing so invites you to move from observing through your inner witness to changing your relationship to what is happening. For example, picture yourself having a chronic, life-long disease, like diabetes. Perhaps you already contend with something chronic or lifelong. You can fight the truth of it, the moment-to-moment experience of it, but it does not change its existence. If you release the struggle against your disease, relief and a sense of empowerment is possible because now you can focus on how to best take care of yourself *given* what is true. I liken it to trying to build a fire in the wind and rain. After many failed attempts, you no longer strain to light that match. Instead, you bundle up in your tent and enjoy watching the fierceness of the storm, warmed in a different way.

Slowing down is another way to practice mindfulness. Notice what happens when you change the pace, like when you slow down your driving and are surprised by how much scenery there is to take in; views that you can't enjoy when you are whizzing by.

Your ability to be with inner pain is also an essential part of being mindful and is an internal resource you can build. You may feel resistant to dealing with pain because you have, until now, believed yourself to be ill-equipped to handle it. However, the question becomes, have you truly tested this belief? Sometimes the idea of pain, which is more of a thought than actual experience, is much harder than dealing with the pain itself. I have sat with clients so afraid to feel their fear, but once they finally do, realize that the terror was much more about their story rather than terror itself. Additionally, your capacity to be with inner pain has only grown since childhood. Given this, even if it *used* to be too much, it may be time to confront an outdated perspective.

Finally, in practicing mindfulness, a curiosity emerges. You become aware that you have spent much of your life predicting and assuming what will happen in the future; this includes the future five minutes from now. When you live in the flow of moments as they unfold, your guesses are just that: guesses. And while you may sometimes be correct in guessing what happens in the future, often you are incorrect – dramatically incorrect.

Think about when you were sure something terrible was going to happen, suffering as you lived with your projections, only to discover that you were wrong. Imagine it this way: you have never been in any moment you are experiencing before now. And even if so much of it is familiar, it is still a new moment. When you are on the river, you have no idea what is around the next bend. Though you may have traversed that same river before, the river could have changed – a tree has fallen, an eagle built a nest, or a beautiful new beach formed. Practicing mindfulness is like that; it's the ongoing discovery of what each moment has to offer.

## *Practice*

1. Start taking in more sensory information around you: sights, smells, sounds, tastes, and even tactile information. Notice body sensations. A focus on your senses keeps your attention on your direct experience of the present moment, which is much easier than relying on your mind to stay interested.

2. Focus on mindfulness in at least two realms of your life, such as being more mindful of your body, while eating, being in nature, driving, etc.

3. Each day, start with a 1-5 minute deep breathing meditation; this will reinforce using breath to bring you back to the present moment throughout the rest of your day. Your breath is like an anchor to the now.

4. Notice those around you who seem particularly present, comfortable with themselves, and able to be with whatever is arising in the moment. How does this happen for them? Consider asking!

5. Change your relationship to time; this is not to encourage lateness, but more about recognizing the sense of franticness so common these days, as many in Western culture have more to do and less time in which to do it. By experiencing time as abundant versus scarce, you can engage more deeply in the moment. A great mantra is: "I have enough time for everything."

6. Become more organized in your life. Disorganization leads to distraction, which interferes with the ability to be mindful and fully present in every moment.

7. Check out "A Good Day" with Brother David Steindl-Rast on YouTube.

8. Listen to "Your Life is Now" by John Mellencamp.

## Stories from the field...

Gerry is not a particularly mindful person; yet. She has a busy mind, mostly set in the future, and primarily focused on "doing" in her life. She is also not a meditator, nor a spiritual practitioner. Gerry has barely even begun to understand, much less experience, a deep sense of being present. But she has experienced a profound moment of it. And that is all it takes. Floating in a pool recently, without any agenda to experience anything at all, she became completely present. There was an absence of thought, especially thoughts of the future, of something to worry about, or something to do. What happened in the intensity of feeling the present moment entirely was a powerful sense of peace, deep relaxation, and expansiveness. She was surprised, in awe, and so grateful. She also wants to experience it again.

The reasonable next step would be to get back into the pool! But for most of us, trying to recreate a moment like that keeps us in a doing versus being place. Gerry would likely be in the pool, trying to re-create her initial experience, thinking the whole time about how not to think. A better next step might be to immerse herself fully in what exists in her life, on a moment-by-moment basis. Her goal is to get out of her head and practice trusting herself and her future more. In a way, she has to completely let go of the moment in the pool that was the very one that inspires her to practice mindfulness. As she does, her full attention is available to experience the present moment.

# *Deepening Mindfulness: Being with Pain*

Knowing how to work with emotional pain is essential if you are to practice mindfulness because it will eventually show up. Repressed emotional pain often begins to surface when you get quiet. This is because your defenses have been quite effective in keeping your inner pain on a shelf. Usually, it goes like this: you know something is there, or a part of you does, but you keep staying three steps ahead of it believing that you are not capable of experiencing it. Remember, the defenses that keep you from feeling pain have been your friend, since you *weren't* as likely to have the inner resources in the past that you do now. So as you deepen your practice of mindfulness, and in that, become willing to face any repressed pain that you carry, don't be surprised if you experience resistance in the form of anxiety. Taking a stance of compassion toward your fear is incredibly beneficial as you move toward any old hurts and heartaches that lie within you.

To work best with your inner pain, you will need to feel resourced, which can be as simple as being rested or as complex as learning to be a comfort to yourself when you are vulnerable. Creating an environment of safety in your inner world, such that when you are vulnerable, you are not judging or shaming those feelings, is also critical. Judging can look like "This isn't that big a deal. So many people have it so much harder" or "My parents did the best they could. I need to get over what happened to me." Imagine how hard it would be to share your struggles with someone if they judged you for struggling. That other person is you on the inside. So instead, imagine your response to yourself and your pain in the way that a dear friend would sit with you: empathetic, present, and curious. The stronger and more loving your relationship to yourself is, as explored in *Aspect One, Befriending You*, the easier it will be to offer comfort to yourself when you are feeling inner pain.

Your ability to challenge untrue thoughts is especially valuable in working with emotional pain. For example, if you have felt lonely from not getting the attention you have needed, saying to yourself "I'm too needy, and people don't like those who are needy" will only make you feel worse and likely prevent you from reaching out to connect. And thoughts like that are untrue. Your feeling of loneliness doesn't make you too needy. Feeling lonely is a human experience that prompts you to connect with others, which is a very healthy response to that particular human need. The point is that it's hard enough to welcome pain and then feel it. Creating more pain with thoughts that go unchallenged is unnecessary and unkind.

As inner pain emerges and needs your attention to heal, you have a choice. The question becomes, "Do I push my pain back down?" or do I finally say, "Yes, I am willing to feel and therefore, heal it." Know that your loving attention is the medicine you need.

Many of us, once we realize this, are excited to start the process. We sit, inviting our repressed pain to show up. Sometimes this works; becoming more mindful does serve as a catalyst. But making space and time for inner pain to surface doesn't always mean that it happens right away. Plan to be patient, imagining that your pain is waiting to see if it can trust you.

In managing my blood disease, I have learned to walk this walk of meeting my pain with love. As mentioned earlier in *Aspect One, Befriending You*, I have a diagnosed blood condition that requires phlebotomies, which is the regular removal of a certain amount of blood. Initially, the procedure was required weekly. All of my life, I have had fear and resistance to needles. With each phlebotomy, I felt anxious and vulnerable. In the beginning, I dismissed my vulnerability and feelings, saying to myself, "What's the big deal? It doesn't even hurt that much, and this is saving your life." What that approach did was skyrocket my anxiety to the point that I was either having a mild panic attack during the phlebotomies or fighting one. But over time, I realized what I was doing and the suffering I was creating for myself. Though my inner witness had helped me tolerate the experience better than before, I was still judging my reaction.

A significant shift happened after this realization. I began to be gentle and kind to myself before, during, and after the weekly procedures. And with that, not surprisingly, the intensity of the experience lessened. Though the difficulty did not altogether disappear, there was softness around the experience that was huge in terms of coping with a reaction I didn't understand. As if being loving and kind in the face of vulnerability with myself wasn't the best of it, not long after this shift an old memory surfaced that explained my deep and visceral reaction to needles. My practice of non-judgment allowed the recollection to appear.

When I was around four years old, I was in a hospital, without either parent, as was the protocol at the time. I had IV's placed in both my thighs that stayed throughout what was a very long night. Alone either in a room or a hallway, I remember screaming in pain and begging for someone to come and take the needles out. I felt unbelievably alone and helpless, which makes my current experience so much more understandable.

Thankfully, I had shifted to a loving posture with myself, which allowed the memory to come through. That memory made sense of my experience and now compels even more compassion for the scared and overwhelmed little girl that was me.

In working with your inner pain, it is essential to know what to do with the emotions themselves when they arise. In a way, it is to do nothing. But doing nothing means you let them wave through, from beginning to end. It's straightforward but new and challenging. Too often emotions are only felt briefly before they are labeled and analyzed.

The idea of "staying with" an emotion is very different. I encourage you to be willing to feel an emotion as a wave that can last minutes but generally won't last hours; especially when you have a disciplined mind that isn't generating new emotions. This process happens with all core feelings, including sadness, anger, fear, and even joy. Knowing the process can help quell the anxiety of being overcome by emotions. And when you experience an emotional wave to completion, a feeling of lightness, calm, and expansion await you on the other side. Working with your emotions in this way correlates directly to you living as your awakened self; this is in contrast to trying to escape uncomfortable emotions through repression, distraction, analysis, or fixing.

What I've described in terms of feeling your emotions all the way through, and feeling better on the other side, is the process of how our healthy brain works. But for those with complex trauma, waves of emotion do not always have an end, or at least the waves of emotion are much longer and more intense. If this is you, it is important not to feel as if you are doing something wrong. If what I offered as a picture in the paragraph above is not your experience, it is a great idea to engage the help of a therapist. Through therapy or programs such as Dialectical Behavior Therapy, you can train yourself to ride the tougher waves.

Before this moment, you may have believed that you couldn't handle certain feelings. And before this moment, as I have been offering, that may have been true. But just as likely, this is an outdated belief, just like the many beliefs you have begun to challenge. On your own or with the help of a therapist, you have and can build a capacity to be with your pain. Remember that your adult capacity to handle pain is greater than your ability as a child. The opportunity here is to build your threshold with the practice of staying with an emotion rather than avoiding it. Doing so enables you to experience intense feelings for longer times with less temptation to escape. And even if you need to take breaks from feeling an emotion all the way through, you are still building your capacity to meet your pain. In those times when a break is needed, lean in, feel as much as you can, and back off. Then, when you are ready, go back to the pain.

The trick to staying with your emotions is to focus on the wave and not your thoughts. Your mind is used to being involved, accustomed to thinking more about emotions than feeling them. The more you *feel* rather than *think,* the faster your mind will settle since there is nothing to do or fix.

As you engage in this practice of staying with your emotions, pay attention to your body, since your body is connected with your feelings. See if you can notice where in your body you feel your emotions. Don't' worry if you can't, but if you can, then, stay with the sensations just like you did with your emotions. If your chest is heavy when you feel sad, imagine just being present with the heaviness. If your stomach feels upset, imagine sitting quietly and lovingly with your upset tummy. Staying with sensations in this way helps them to subside. Finally, be aware of images that arise. Maybe fear is a vice or sadness looks like a heavy cloak. Those kinds of images are powerful. Similar to emotion and sensation, you can simply be present with the image. In doing so, perhaps the vice loosens, or the cloak that is pressing against your chest becomes a blanket that comforts.

Wonderfully, when you are fully present with your emotions, you will often be gifted with insights that drop into your lap like a delicious ripe fruit that falls from the tree. Clarity comes from that place of calm expansiveness on the other side of an emotional wave. You don't have to think yourself into wisdom; instead, it emerges naturally as part of this process.

Know that this process of staying with your emotions invites other feelings to arise. You may discover deeper emotions hidden underneath the original feeling you had, such as disappointment under anger or loneliness under sadness. For example, my anger at my parent's divorce was both the anger of feeling blamed by my father and the shame that accompanied that blame; but at a deeper level, my pain was about my profound grief in losing him.

## Practice

To heal your pain is to have access to it. Below, I offer several ways to begin. Before engaging with any of the ideas I describe, make sure have the resources to do so. That may mean you are rested and comfortable. It may mean not doing it alone or that you wait until you are not at a time in your life where there is a lot of stress or change. Remember also, as you travel this part of the river, who you are is bigger than the pain itself. The love that you are holds the pain that you feel. Begin with your inner witness by your side, which can help you from becoming overwhelmed.

1. Start with a centering and calming ritual, such as deep breathing or meditation. Keep yourself relaxed as you gently invite your pain to be present.

2. Reflect upon any pain you carry. Go as deep as you can, exploring what layers exist, and what is primary. Ask how old is it and whether there is an emotional theme such as fear, regret, shame, anger, loneliness, sadness, or desperation?

3. Close your eyes and drop inside and see what you find after a few moments. If any pain bubbles up, like feelings of sadness, anger, fear, or loneliness, imagine yourself comforting that pain. If inner pain doesn't come up easily or immediately, be patient. Your pain may be locked away and need a series of gentle urgings to come out. And remember, often deep and old pain is repressed because it was too much to feel when you

were younger. Because of this, pain can be initially difficult to access. However, over time, with a practice of sitting and inviting, your pain will likely begin to surface. Keep in mind that right now, in this process, you have resources that you didn't have as a child. Like a shy child longing to be coaxed into a warm embrace, though initially reluctant, your defenses melt in an environment of love.

4.  Stay with your pain without attempts to figure it out, fix, or reject it; this is like the warrior dropping the shield, and standing strong in the vulnerability of feeling. As you do this, privilege all emotions, allowing your anger or your disgust to be as important to you as your joy and your peace. If resistance occurs, focus on loving the resistance, the protective part of you afraid to feel. Let it be okay that you aren't ready. Sometimes, honoring the resistance softens it like a cube of butter in the warm sunshine. By staying with your emotions, new doors open up, and when honoring all feelings, including your defenses as a form of fear, something deep within you shifts and transforms. The possibility here is incredible.

5.  Take a picture from your childhood, and begin to have a conversation with this child, speaking from your heart. What good do you see within this child? What pain? What does this child need to hear and what does this child need to say? To whom? What do you see when you look into your young eyes? How long has it been since you connected to this young version of yourself? The pain you have carried may be clearer as you look at your younger self.

    Your willingness to allow all emotions to come forward is the best medicine you can offer this child. In this process, it is about feeling what shut down before.

6. If you don't want to use an actual picture, create a picture in your imagination: you sitting on a park bench as your adult, current self together with your younger, child self. Maybe you talk, and if so, below I offer some ideas. But maybe you are just present with your pain, sitting with an arm around this younger, injured part of you.

    Healing your pain can be about offering to yourself what you didn't get as a child: your loving presence as well as the loving messages that you yearned for and the retraction of any messages that injured or frightened you. Here is an example of words you could offer:

    "You are lovable, you belong, you matter, and you are safe. Right here and now, I see your pain, your hurts, and I see your innocence. I see your heart. I see you." There may be even more specific words, such as, "You are enough," "You are not stupid," "You are so wanted," or even, "It wasn't really about you at all." Why is it important that *you* find the words instead of someone else? Because you know best what you needed to hear. Looking to your partner, children, a friend, or the world to heal is like going out in the world with a cup that has holes. As soon as you get what you need (love, acceptance, belonging), it can drain out the holes, over and over again. When you come to understand that you have, within yourself, so much of what you have searched for, the holes begin to fill.

7. Imagine sharing your pain with another person, a close friend, a partner, or a therapist. Part of healing is to know you are not alone, and in being vulnerable, you not only undo aloneness, but it may take your relationship with that person to another level.

8. Listen to "Touch That Fire" by Vicci Martinez.

9.  Consider forgiveness work. Below are three beginning steps to three substantial pieces of personal work. Though no small thing to dive into, forgiveness is part of healing inner pain and is essential to fully living as your awakened self. Start with one of the three. Consider journaling or talking with someone about how you can make it happen. It may mean, for example, working on communication or repairing an injury before asking for forgiveness from another. In terms of forgiving yourself, it may involve a greater degree of self-acceptance to make forgiving your mistakes possible.

    a.  ask for forgiveness

    b.  forgive yourself

    c.  choose to forgive another

### Stories from the field...

As he looked at his picture, Nicolas couldn't stop crying. He felt the innocence of a child that, unbeknownst to this child he stared at, life was about to give a gut punch of intense trauma, loss, and pain. It hurt to remember and to see his innocence before the trauma occurred. And the loss of innocence was only the tip of the iceberg of the pain that Nicolas carried. Distrust, self-hatred, and utter loneliness were the impacts of his boyhood wounds. Connecting with the child that *experienced* the trauma and loss resulted in a level of re-experiencing it. But Nicolas was brave. He chose to release the pain he had held for so long, the pain that had stood in the way of the happiness and peace he sought. As he broke down, he broke free of his pain. Being in touch with the pain allowed him to see that many of his beliefs and stories about himself and the world were born out of circumstances he had no control over. He saw that his patterns of destruction came from these beliefs. Ultimately, the truth saved him. He began to recognize that the beliefs were not his. They were untrue. Expressing his pain and seeing his narrative as false were both a part of living as his awakened self. His tears became tears of relief and gratitude as he realized that his pain sourced his addictive drinking and compulsive behavior. As he healed, what was his pathology became part of his cherished path of waking up and becoming whole.

## Mindfulness and Relationship

Do you remember falling in love with something or someone – romantic love that burst on the scene, the birth of a newborn baby, or a newly discovered place in nature? You were probably in a state of full presence and didn't have to work at being mindful. What was in front of you consumed you because it was new and powerful. But what happens when what or who is in front of you is not new? Do you, like many, find yourself less interested and more easily distracted?

Mindfulness is about being in the current moment and not predicting the next. With longer term relationships, or where you have stereotypes, it is easy to think you can predict what is going to be said or done next. However, when you pay more attention to your predictions rather than the person in front of you, you have lost your way in your relationships. This lack of relational mindfulness has a significant impact. When you are not entirely present with another, there is a painful lack of connection, as well as the loss of what could have been.

To explore the practice of mindfulness in a relationship, I invite you first to feel the consequence of its absence. Notice what it feels like to be on the receiving end of distraction. It doesn't feel good. One of the most debilitating human experiences is that of being ignored, completely or even partially. When this happens to you, your brain becomes destabilized, and your sense of well-being can break down. Given this, it is no wonder feeling shunned or invisible is devastating and can send you into a tailspin.

The practice of mindfulness gives to others the opposite experience: that of feeling visible and important to you. As we explored in *Aspect Two, Freedom from your Mind*, when you can challenge your projections of others, it clears the stories of your mind that interfere with being present. The practice of mindfulness adds to this; when you aren't distracted, the connection is even stronger, and the message of "You are important to me" even more evident.

While this sounds great, for some, practicing mindfulness in relationships can be challenging. Being fully present in a relationship is emotionally intimate. And this form of intimacy can be uncomfortable. When this is true, whether it is because intimacy is unfamiliar or there is distrust due to an injury, it is essential to accept that discomfort will be part of practicing relational mindfulness.

To overcome discomfort, start with a focus on slowing down, making more eye contact, and staying in your body. Over time, your consistency in practicing relational mindfulness will decrease discomfort and offers greater ease and confidence with intimacy.

For those who fear intimacy because there is a history of being hurt by others, practicing mindfulness in a relationship and the vulnerability that follows can be much harder. And though resistance to intimacy is understandable when there have been injuries, there is still a high price to pay: loss of meaningful connection, loneliness, and mostly living in an old paradigm.

If there is a way to directly repair any injuries with someone who has hurt you, explore the idea of doing so. *Aspect Seven, Conscious Relationships* has a tool specifically focused on repairing injuries that can help. When you can't repair an injury with the person that hurt you, plan on being patient with yourself as you learn to open up to others. You will need to make it safe again to experience intimacy. Part of doing that is to make injuries relationship-specific and not overgeneralize.

Given that mindfulness is about being with all that is true, this means not only facing the discomfort of intimacy and repairing injuries but any other hard stuff, such as when there is an issue or concern. It is about being willing to move toward, rather than away from, conflict or difficulty. Examples of this are a change in compatibility or a hurt, be it with a friend or significant other. You can ignore what is true and drift away, or you can pivot toward what is difficult and navigate your way through.

You may have been taught by your family of origin to avoid conflict. If so, you would have learned to work at ignoring what was in the moment when there was a problem. While growing up, and even looking back, that tactic may have seemed to work. It kept the peace, in a certain kind of way. But here's the deal: what needs resolution remains stuck, what needs healing continues to be a wound, and the potential of the relationship to rise to the occasion of addressing difficult things remains unrealized.

Facing difficulty takes courage. Without knowing how to proceed, it is easy to let fear be in charge. While your nervous system might like it if you avoid difficulties and refrain from being mindful, your heart does not. Since curiosity can help quell fear, imagine being curious about the gifts of mindfulness and your capacities as more significant than your fear of the potential conflict. Picture saying to yourself, "I wonder how this will unfold when I am fully present and bring my whole self to the table? Perhaps I will be delighted, surprised, and maybe even relieved. What would it be like to hold me and my relationships capable of practicing mindfulness?" What if, in the cases of injury or incompatibility, you and the other person find healing and new ways to be together? What if the other person has been yearning for the same resolution and a deeper connection?

When two people decide to take the plunge into the scary waters of addressing a concern or a hurt so that they can be fully present with one another, if handled well, astonishing things can happen. Instead of a relationship that is threatened by truth and vulnerability, the connection gets stronger and closer. Each person can end up feeling a sense of competence and confidence in the shared ability to work with adversity. The result is magical. No longer do you have to pretend, distract, or turn away from what is present. Instead, practicing mindfulness in the face of difficulty opens up the possibility that no matter what arises in the moment, you've got what it takes to navigate tricky waters together.

Ultimately, by facing any resistance you have toward intimacy and dealing with the hard stuff, you promote living as your awakened self, which is not distracted or hidden behind walls of protection. It is about bringing your whole self forward. Mindfulness is more than just being in the moment; it is having *all* of you there. As I mentioned above, in *Aspect Seven, Conscious Relationships*, I offer tools and practices that can help with the process. Remember, mindfulness is like the swimming hole of the river. When you practice mindfulness in your relationships, you have invited another to swim in the beautiful waters with you.

## Practice

1. In practicing relational mindfulness, go slowly when fear of rejection or judgment is present. Carefully choose who you open up to in terms of practicing mindfulness in your relationships since you are in the process of rebuilding trust in others. It might be as simple as making longer eye contact or slowing down your interactions, which include your speech

and the way you listen. Starting there may build a better foundation by which to attempt resolution and repair later.

2.  Stay current and accurate in your relationships. Challenge your projections. Ask yourself, "How much of my perception is laced with ideas and experiences from the past or even from not having enough information? What may have changed and would I notice if it did?"

3.  Within a partnered relationship, try one of these:

    *   Start each day with several moments of silence together. Notice what happens when you stop and are present with one another for the moment.

    *   Consider having a conversation about anything that needs attention in the relationship; this will help you to stay current in the relationship and not caught up in unresolved concerns of the past.

### Stories from the field . . .

Annie and Chris loved each other very much and treated each other with kindness and respect. Together for almost ten years, they spent their 20's establishing a life in Oregon. But over time, they stopped paying attention. They were on autopilot, coasting along until a difficult event woke them up. Their relationship was mostly driven by function and habit, keeping them each unaware of how doing so endangered their relationship. So they started paying attention. Both got honest with themselves and each other and began to deal with long-term resentments, hurts, and the detachment that had begun to define them as a couple. And though they did not know where practicing mindfulness would lead them, they trusted and courageously welcomed all of what was present and true. On the other side of a crisis that ultimately became transformation, they know now that being distracted or dismissive of what is happening in their relationship isn't an option. As they enjoy a relationship that is far more real and honest, practicing mindfulness has become the new habit. Annie and Chris bring forth their awakened selves to a relationship that is teeming with aliveness.

# Aspect Four

## Cherishing Your Body

If the river is your human journey, flowing toward the vast expanse of the ocean, then your body is the vessel that gets you there. In exploring some of the facets of your inner world so far, we've already connected your emotions to your body. Now, we take a deeper dive into cherishing your body as part of living as your awakened self.

It's pretty hard to be in the flow of wakefulness when you are suffering from a hangover, or you overdid exercise. It's difficult to have loving self-talk when you are mad at yourself or suffering the consequences of neglect or self-harm. Think about the many miles a river must travel to the ocean. Water in the boat, an engine that doesn't work well, or even a craft that is too cumbersome to traverse the narrows ahead effectively; each of these dramatically impacts the journey. So then is your voyage affected if you have a body that is compromised.

Just like being disconnected from your emotions, it is possible to be disconnected from your body. You might feed it and get it dressed, but you don't have a relationship to it. If this describes you, it is likely you are living in disconnection from the very vessel in which you travel. Your first step in cherishing your body is to choose a relationship where your sense of self includes feeling present in and connected to your body.

Once you have decided to have an active relationship to your body, there may be hurdles to overcome, including messages about your body from the world, society, and even your family. The culture in which most of us live can have lots of ideas and views that may or may not align with the body you or I have.

In many cultures, there is a body type that is considered ideal. Few have it, and without interventions like surgery, those that have it can't keep it. Something is always too big or too small, too soft or not fit enough, skin that is not clear enough or hair that is too gray; the list goes on and on. So in cherishing your body, after you establish that you have a relationship to it, you are tasked with accepting your body as imperfect. Not that your body, the human body, isn't magnificent. It is. It's just not perfect.

Self-acceptance around your body usually shows up in the quality and content of your self-talk; what you say to yourself that no one else hears. For those who live in a culture where appearance is based on ideas of perfection, with a message of shame for having an imperfect body, it is easy to have harsh and critical inner dialogue. The voice of the culture becomes the voice in your head. The lack of acceptance by others becomes the rejection of your body. To embrace your body as imperfect takes tremendous courage; it means you are brave enough to emancipate yourself from the mindset of a perfectionistic culture and decide that perfection is both unattainable *and* undesirable. Taking this new mindset into your inner world heals the pain of shame. In cherishing your body, you give yourself relief from the effort and anxiety in attempting to fight your body's imperfections.

From here, we delve into three components of cherishing your body: appreciating your body, taking care of your body, and exploring body harm and neglect.

All relationships benefit from acknowledgment and appreciation. Your relationship with your body is no different. Imagine feeling grateful for what your body does functionally to keep you alive, as well as its capacity to absorb stress, experience emotions, and deal with trauma. Your appreciation of each and all of these can revolutionize your relationship. Often, the more you understand all that your body does, the greater respect you will have for it.

In terms of understanding the human system, science has only scratched the surface. Much of what happens in your body does so without any effort or awareness on your part. Your body keeps trucking along without you needing to do or know very much. While you are busy living your life, your body is busy fighting disease and generating new cells. And when stressed, your body takes in what it experiences, good or bad, much like a sponge that absorbs water, whether it's muscle tightness as a response to stress or an upset stomach due to anxiety.

In realizing how much your body does *for* you, not only might you be feeling grateful, you may also start feeling protective; this is a good thing. When grateful, you will be less inclined to take your body for granted. When protective, you are more apt to take excellent care of your body. The second component of living consciously in your body, taking care of it, naturally happens when you are protective. Taking care of your body can go far beyond getting regular exercise and maintaining a healthy weight. Something as simple as using the restroom when you need to without postponement is a small but profound action in allowing what your body needs to matter to you. Taking action like this means taking *really* good care, rather than doing the bare minimum; listening instead of dismissing what your body is communicating to you.

When you ignore what you hear, your body suffers, even if it is just a little. Your body is part of the whole system that is you. Notice how often you minimize what your body is telling you. Maybe that takes form in not responding to needing food or sleep. The hope is that the more protective you become, the harder it gets to ignore and dismiss your physical needs. In being attuned to your body, it's like you've become a radio dispatcher that stays tuned in to what's going on, responding with love and urgency to what your body needs and wants.

But responding to what your body is saying is challenging if the lines of communication are broken or faint. If so, consider having a dialogue with your body to see what it needs. The best way to start the conversation with your body is to ask, "If my body could talk to me, what would it say?" Then listen. So often, your body has been waiting for you to pose this very question and is happy to give you honest and quick feedback.

Here is an example of listening to the body. A few years back, I heard "stop running" as what my body was saying to me, which was the last thing I wanted to hear. Immediately, I felt fear. Then sadness showed up for the potential loss of a 40-year tradition of being a runner. This beloved practice was much more meaningful than the fitness it provided. Running was part of how I defined myself. It also helped me to maintain my mental health.

Further, when I traveled, running was my way of exploring different cultures, and at home, experiencing nature. But I kept listening to what my body was saying and stayed with the process. After the fear settled down, and I moved through the sadness, I watched my ego try to negotiate. Would I get as much respect if I weren't a runner? Would my body change and would others judge if it did? I continued to work with my resistance such that eventually, I was able to quit running altogether. Because I worked with my fear and stayed steadfast in my willingness to listen, I eventually relaxed into life as a non-runner. Though I missed running, I was not afraid. I stopped without any sense that I would ever run again. From time to time, I would check in with my body. To my surprise, and after a long sabbatical, I began to hear something new; a stirring that was not fear, nor compulsion. A stirring that eventually said to me, "Run, but run differently." Now, as a runner, it *is* different; I run less often, and I don't track miles. If injured, I don't run at all. Increasingly, I stretch. Mostly, I run with gratitude and less fear, enjoying this form of movement without feeling addicted. In doing so, my body knows it can trust me to listen to it.

Sometimes, appreciating your body, as well as taking better care through healthier practices and improved listening, is not enough. You may need to go a step further because you have been mistreating your body, doing things that cause actual harm. While exploring the third component of living consciously in your body, know that neglect or damage can be dramatic or subtle. Harm can look like binging on alcohol, drugs, or food. Harm can also be not regularly seeing a doctor as a form of neglect, or over-exercising based on the false belief that a healthy behavior in excess can't hurt you. Any type of neglect or harm counts because the message to your body is the same: "I will hurt you. You are not safe with me."

Breaking habits and stopping self-harming behaviors can be difficult, especially those habits and practices that have existed for years. As mentioned before, the longer something exists in time and is repeated, the more ingrained it is in the brain, which can show up as resistance to change, even if that change is desperately wanted. Changing long-standing habits can even feel impossible and the idea paralyzing.

So how can you stop years and sometimes decades of neglect or self-harm? At least some of the answer lies in your willingness to take stock and feel the impact of your choices. Taking stock means you fully face the consequences of what you do every day that results in injury or suffering for your body. As you take an inventory, start by noticing how it *feels* to be making those choices. Be prepared to feel uncomfortable as you break out of denial. By doing so, even before you've made any changes, change is happening through your increased awareness and honesty; no longer do you "get away with" what you do or don't do that hurts your body.

Let your uneasiness be motivating. The stronger your discomfort, the stronger your motivation and thus the easier it will be to deal with impulses for self-harm and habits that have a stronghold. There is a saying, called "surf the urge". As an urge or an impulse rises inside of you to do something harmful to your body, imagine it as a wave. Like an emotion, a wave of impulse has a beginning, middle, and most importantly, an end. As you patiently ride out the wave, know that the urge is temporary, and your body is safe.

In terms of how you treat your body, it is also motivating to consider who is watching the choices that you are making. If you are a parent, your kids are your audience. If you teach, your students are your witness. If you are in a partnership, your partner is the one who sees what you do. Mistreating your body in front of others doesn't feel great and therefore gives you the push you might need to do something different. Know that the more transparent you are with others, in contrast to hiding your mistreatment, the greater the inclination to take better care. Lastly, what you do not only matters for you, but consider that in mistreating your body, you are potentially teaching others to do the same.

If you continue to have trouble with neglecting or harming your body, consider enlisting a professional counselor. Self-harm and neglect can stem from significant and complex trauma that has not been resolved or healed. In these cases, such as an eating disorder that can become life-threatening, willpower will not be enough, and failed attempts not to hurt or neglect can result in shame and feelings of despair. A skilled and compassionate therapist can help pull the pieces together, which can result in your ability to create and sustain change.

In summary, cherishing your body builds a foundation of acceptance and appreciation, shifting from neglect or harm to gratitude and protection. Working with your inner self-talk and outer choices and behaviors offers a holistic experience of living consciously in your body. Imagine hearing a voice in your head that doesn't say what is wrong, but instead celebrates your body's beauty and all that it does for you. Picture a reality in which *you* get to set the standards by which you see and experience your body. Maybe this would be embracing your wrinkles as pleasing because they represent living, loving, and laughing; or loving a body that can birth a baby with the belly that held that baby bigger and softer than before. As your awakened self, you travel in a vessel well-loved and cared for, seen for its complexity, generosity, and beauty.

## Practice

1. Journal the following questions:

   - How do I feel about my body?

   - Do I fully understand and appreciate all that my body does for me?

   - What do I say to my body? What is my inner dialogue?"

   - How do I treat my body and do I ignore its cues or mistreat it in any way?

2. The answers to these questions will likely offer what you need to heal. Perhaps it will be with your self-talk as you look in the mirror. Maybe it will be in listening to your body. Perhaps it will be as simple as having a relationship with your body.

3. Complete the Body Image exercise on page 93.

4. Commit to accepting your body and working with any pain/shame you carry.

5. Consider hugging yourself from time to time. Like a touch from a good friend, a self-embrace can create much of the

same feeling, especially as you deepen your relationship with yourself.

6.  Engage in bodywork, such as massage, acupuncture, or chiropractic. These modalities offer a way to release stress from the body.

7.  If you are working with a psychotherapist, ask whether or not they can include somatic-experiencing work, which means they work with you in increasing body awareness and attunement, especially around how the body experiences emotion.

8.  Write a letter of amends to your body.

# Body Image Worksheet

1. Do you believe any part of your body to be overweight, unattractive, or unhealthy?

2. When and from whom did you get that message?

3. Did either parent struggle with body image?

4. What do you say to yourself when you look in the mirror?

5. How much time, preoccupation, and focus does your body take up in your inner world?

6. If you could be free from a story, projected upon by you or by others about your body, would you want that? Will freedom from the story be about changing your body or changing your mindset?

7. What would your inner dialogue be if you were to change your mindset? What would you say to yourself, especially as you look in the mirror?

8. How transparent are you with your partner about how you feel about your body?

9. Do you believe that if you accept your body as imperfect and flawed something bad will happen, such as you will stop taking care of it or be unloved, rejected, or judged by another?

   If this resonates with you, I encourage you to face your fears. Use your work in *Aspect Two, Freedom from your Mind* as a way to challenge any thoughts or beliefs you have that interfere with accepting your body.

## *Stories from the field . . .*

Grant is fit and takes excellent care of his body. In many ways, he has stayed ahead of the typical aging process for a man his age. But for many years, he carried shame around his body; shame in particular in regards to his belly. His attempts to hide what felt shameful meant that he lived in a constant state of holding in his belly. The anxiety and physical stress had become so normal that he didn't even notice doing it. But as Grant is waking up and cherishing his body, he sees his shame and pain much more clearly. His judgments toward his body have roots to his past, as well as being the result of living in his culture. He saw that he could try harder to change this part of his body, and perhaps experience some decrease in shame. But his real work was to accept his body as imperfect and emancipate from the culture and conditioning. Grant began being more interested in cherishing his body rather than living in the strain and anxiety of constantly holding in his belly. He started to heal the shame he carried by challenging his judgment. If you saw Grant today, you would celebrate. He can be shirtless and much more relaxed in allowing others to see his belly. He enjoys kinder self-talk as a result of accepting his body as imperfect. And for those around him, he reflects a true state of grace in living in his body with respect and dignity.

# Aspect Five
## Embracing Death & Dying

*"We all have two lives and the second begins
when we realize we only have one." ~ Confucius*

Each river eventually arrives at the ocean, just as each of us
ultimately reaches the moment of death. Most of us don't spend
much time contending with the end of life until we get nearer to it
or until someone close passes away. Too often, when it's not
about us, we go back to ignoring the reality of our demise.

What if you turned toward your death, not because you've lost
someone or because it is upon you but because you are interested
in the peace that would be yours by doing so? Long before
experiencing death, changing your relationship to that which you
travel toward changes the journey in getting there; how powerful
it would be, then, to experience less fear, more relaxation, and
even curious anticipation about one of the inevitabilities of life.

For many, the difficulty in facing death is more about the
potential dying process than it is about death itself. The fear of pain
or disability that can accompany death can be scary to confront. If
this is true for you, then see if you can keep the two – death and
dying – separate. Thankfully, at least some of the time and with
some illnesses, pain management options are available that didn't
exist before. Knowing and remembering this can quell some of the
fear around the dying process.

You may have avoided facing death because you did not feel
ready, it felt too intense, or maybe it just seemed quite far off.
Maybe you have been afraid to face it because of fears of a difficult
afterlife. Perhaps you have felt entitled to living a certain number

of years or having specific life experiences. If you have not come to terms with death and dying, for these or any other reasons, you are not alone. Waiting to deal with death and dying until you have to works in a certain sense; you get to avoid what is difficult until you have no other choice but to do so. But there is a price, which includes missing out on the gifts available in embracing death and dying. If avoidance has been your path or position, I urge you to do something different. Imagine it as deciding to go down the rapids instead of choosing to walk along the shore.

One of the gifts in accepting death is experiencing less anxiety around it. With less anxiety comes more energy. In Daniel's story from the field on page 103, he offers "I have found that the fear of death is tiring; it steals energy." Death, of course, is a part of life, whether you accept it or not, pay attention to it or not, and ultimately, like it or not. And it keeps getting closer. If you've avoided coming to terms with this, over time, you have to work harder to distract yourself from this reality. That distraction takes energy even though it maintains the illusion that death can be kept at arm's length. So when you stop distracting, there is a sense of relief and a greater sense of vitality.

In sitting with those facing death, not as a potential, but as a reality that is happening, I often wish I could invite others into the room. Daniel's story gives you a taste of what I mean. Each time, I have been deeply moved as I witness fear morph into strength and courage as my clients unearth within them what was needed to navigate their experience. What was terrifying before, such as, "I could never handle having cancer" or "I don't know what I would do if I knew I was going to die" became "I am doing this; it's not at all what I expected" and even in a few cases, "There is so much good in this process." They were relieved by their capacities and resilience, and so often a whole new aliveness ensued: deeper connections with others, more significant presence and clarity, and much less fear about living life on life's terms.

In facing your mortality, you also get to explore what a meaningful life means to you. With measured time, there can be greater intention around the life you are living today. Wakeful living is all about living intentionally, and breaking the illusion that you have unlimited time offers the gift of wisely choosing what you will do with the time you have.

As we have explored, redefining who you are provides much in living as your awakened self. In terms of death and dying, your expanded definition can change the whole experience, since resistance to death is often based on the sense of finality. If you have redefined yourself as part of something vast and eternal, then there is something that doesn't die when your human death occurs. Your body is done. Your human journey is complete. But if there is more, and you are more, the essence of you lives on. In death, like the river, you have arrived at the ocean as part of it.

As you consider the gifts of turning toward your death, consider moving closer to it by creating an image of death and dying. Your image could look something like you sitting in a circle of love with others, calm and beaming, with any fear as an image right next to you, perhaps as a dark, scary cloud. Then, without judging your fear, simply notice that it is not the only thing going on. Appreciate, if you can, that as you sit with both, side-by-side, you are coming to terms with death in a new way. Notice if in doing this, your fear and resistance soften. Without resistance to your resistance, there is often a shift. In this way of being with it, you are beginning to embrace death and dying.

When you are ready to move *even closer*, engage your practice of mindfulness, your ability to challenge your thoughts, and your willingness to be present with your feelings. Doing so will help you to embrace your death further, and gift you with the likelihood of meeting it with more grace and less fear. As you face your death and dying, you have a greater capacity to face the experience itself when it is time. And unless you are literally taking your last breath, you aren't, meaning that you are only dealing with the idea of death, not the direct experience of it.

Know that in facing your death, one of the feelings that may show up is sadness for those you will leave behind when you die. Accepting death can be hard, given the impact on others, especially where there is a lot of love. As it goes, the deeper the love, the greater the loss when you die. But if you can reframe loss as a testament to the amount of love that existed, it will help because profound loss equals profound love. Reframing grief doesn't mean it hurts any less, but it gives a powerful context within which to feel that pain. Then, in our broken-heartedness, the love is felt too, for you and for those you leave behind.

Consider sharing this idea with those you love, such as your children, a partner, or a friend. Tell them, "If I die first, remember that the amount of pain you will feel is about how much love we shared, and loving each other less was never an option." Also keep in mind that the ones you love have innate capacities to move through the grieving process, just as you do. We are all wired to feel and release pain and to recover from our losses. In grieving, what starts as "I wasn't ready to say goodbye" and "I can't imagine life going on" changes over time. The pain shifts from searing to bearable as our broken heart heals. Those who are left at our passing learn to live with the sadness that arises from time to time as part of love and loss.

Ultimately, I invite you to befriend death. Whether you do or don't, it certainly isn't going away. But your friendship with it throws a wide net, offering the many gifts mentioned above. Resistance to this non-negotiable part of life keeps you stuck in an eddy, rather than letting the reality of death be part of the current that takes you to that ocean toward which you travel. In saying "Yes" to death and dying you have come to accept the impermanence of life and time that you can't get back.

Death, as a friend, becomes a welcomed and even celebrated part of life as it helps you to live an awakened one. It is part of the current that you feel beneath you, keeping you connected to the preciousness of life and time. Try exploring these questions: "Does my life have purpose?" or "If I died today, what unfinished business do I have?" and most importantly, "Am I living life fully and as a reflection of who I really am?" Doing so could mean that you finally get your life in order, whether it is as simple as having a current will, or on a bigger scale, changing careers or practicing greater love and authenticity in your relationships. In embracing death and dying, you can live the words, "In my extraordinary life, it is never a good day to die, but just as true, in a life well lived, every day is a good day to die." My hope is that you find within you the courage to make peace with death and dying, and in doing so, discover a new level of living wakefully in your inner world. The following poem by Kahlil Gibran reflects this so beautifully.

## The Prophet

*You would know the secret of death.*
*But how shall you find it unless you seek it in the heart of life?*
*The owl whose night-bound eyes are blind unto the day*
*cannot unveil the mystery of light.*
*If you would indeed behold the spirit of death,*
*open your heart wide unto the body of life.*
*For life and death are one, even as the river and the sea are one.*

*For what is it to die, but to stand naked in the wind*
*and to melt into the sun?*
*And what is it to cease breathing,*
*but to free the breath from its restless tides,*
*That it may rise and expand and seek God unencumbered?*

*Only when you drink from the river of silence shall you indeed sing.*
*And when you have reached the mountaintop, then you shall begin to climb.*
*And when the earth shall claim your limbs, then shall you truly dance.*

## Practice

1.  Sit in meditation with the topic of death. Journal if it is helpful to write. Reflect upon what death means to you and perhaps what teachings or spiritual perspectives resonate with you. Reflect upon your fears of dying. Ask yourself if you are more concerned with death or with dying?

    Additionally, contemplate what you need to do or say to die with a sense of freedom and peace. Do it, even if it means forgiving someone you haven't forgiven, making amends where you have not expressed remorse, or completing something in your life that feels unfinished – your version of a "bucket list".

2.  Revisit the losses you have experienced already in life. Do they feel complete in terms of your grieving, and if not, what would help you finish?

3.  Review obituaries in the paper; try to find those who are your age or near to it. The intent of this is to make death part of life and your death a stronger reality. Then write your obituary. What do you want it to say? You can even go a step further and start planning your funeral.

4.  Visit a graveyard and imagine that these are not graves but people on the same human journey as you. See if you can connect on some level with those buried.

5.  Read a book about death: *A Year to Live*, by Steven Levine, *Making Friends with Death*, by Judith L. Lief, or *I Wasn't Ready to Say Goodbye*, by Brook Noel and Pamela Blair, Ph.D.

6.  Watch the movie, *Harold and Maude*.

7.  Check out Allen Watts' YouTube video on *Death and Dying and Staying Awake*.

## *Stories from the field . . .*

David didn't expect to contend with the premature death of his beautiful and healthy wife. Nor did she. Theresa was a strong and independent woman and had years of a stable and loving marriage with David that included a daughter. When the cancer diagnosis came in, and in the months and years that followed, each rose powerfully to meet the most significant event of their lives, which was her inevitable death. What was stunning was their honesty with each other and with their daughter. Their honesty with themselves was also so touching. Theresa didn't want to pursue a bucket list. Her life embodied her bucket. The road to her passing was virtually no different than the path that she already traveled. And David got to be her companion in the decisions and choices that represented that path. So they didn't stop working. They came into couples counseling to deal with issues, communication, regular "couples therapy" stuff that only *included* her impending death.

After her passing, David turned his grief back into providing support to others who were going or had gone through a similar loss. For David, he reports that support group participation is the most "real" part of his week, week after week. For him, it has become about staying present with the idea of life and death and normalizing the fact that this is part of all of our experience. It is therapeutic for David, and he hopes, for all that come to the support groups.

♦

Fran always said that she wasn't afraid to die. She was steadfast in her belief that there was something beyond death including loved ones waiting for her. Fran didn't believe in a traditional heaven, but reported regularly being in contact with those "on the other side"; this must have been part of her unwillingness to give up her vices, and so, she drank and smoked leading right up to her final days. She refused to let fear change her way of being and her right to make those choices. As a parent, Fran introduced her children to her perspective, which was a huge gift in quelling childhood fears of death. I am one of those children. Throughout all the years of hearing her convictions and exploring aspects of death, such as going to psychics, seeing the movie *Harold and Maude* many, many times, attending funerals at an early age, and hearing her stories of my dead grandma's communication with her, I saw her fearlessness around death. But it is one thing to believe something, to "know it is true" as she would say, and another thing to test it out, so to speak, when the time comes.

This year, Fran died. The time had come to see if her ability to embrace death and dying would see her through. In what was a two-week process, we got to see, first hand, that it did. On one of the nights that we thought was the last, she lay in a hospital bed, without fear, saying, "I am ready, I love you and goodbye." The days prior were filled with stories, laughter, and deep connection. That night, as she drifted off, my sisters and I sang many of her favorite songs. We dozed off at around 3 am, not expecting to see her alive again. Much to everyone's surprise, mostly hers, she woke up the next morning. Her first words were, "What are you all doing here?" and we had a great laugh. Several days later she passed, still with no fear. Wildly, given the great love and sometimes great challenge we had with one another, I was the one with her. The hours leading up to her final breath, unable to see or speak, I would moisten her lips with water; I felt like a mama bird feeding my baby, as my mom turned her face and open mouth toward me. Having embraced her death and dying, she died in peace, able to leave her body and travel to that place and to people for which she yearned.

◆

"I've been active and healthy my whole life, spending a lot of time outdoors. Then, 16 months ago I was diagnosed with terminal cancer. Available treatments are limited; the unknown is how many months I have remaining before I die.

My life changed, not on the external side but the internal, the very personal side of things. My perspectives shifted and my curiosity about life, death, humans, the natural world, and a range of unknown aspects of being suddenly swelled. The reality of dying unleashed a whole new level of wakefulness and being present. It has come to feel as much a physiological shift as an emotional and spiritual shift. My body and mind seem to guide my energy more and more toward the now, the moment.

I have found that the fear of death is tiring; it steals energy, especially that deep energy that I need to get "through the rapids". I can control the fear that shrouds death; I can protect my energy and my spirit by accepting the reality of my condition. The cancer is a part of me, a condition that evolved in my ecosystem. It is up to me to be with it, know it, and co-exist with it. The diagnosis gave me a wonderful sense of life's beauty, its preciousness, and its impermanence. Knowing that time is shortening brings a real sense of what is important, what warrants my energy, my attention. My intentions will bring the moments that make up a day. Then, it turns out that all I really control is my ability to be truly in this moment, the "right now".

At our family Christmas dinner this year I told the family that, though it sounds odd, this last year has been one of the best years of my life."

# Bridging Your Inner and Outer World

So now it's time to move from your inner world to your outer world. And just as the dawn breaks with a new day, you are invited to shift your attention with the same ease, curious about what lies outside of you. The hope is that having found a greater flow of wakefulness in your inner world, you take that flow and find the same in your outer world. The starting place you've cultivated to greet your outer world is a powerful one: a stronger relationship to yourself and your body, with greater freedom from your mind, resting in a mindful way of being, and feeling more resolved around your death and dying.

The first encounter with the outer world is with nature in the form of the air you breathe. From there, you encounter fellow humans. The next two *Aspects* follow this sequence. We then delve into the waters of community, culture, and the world at large, as well as exploring your relationship to a spiritual path and your contribution to the world in which you live.

# Part Two

# The Outer World

# Aspect Six
## Nature as You

Right now, take a big breath, one that fills your whole body. That breath, which sustains your body, also brings a part of your outer world into you. Most of us never really think about nature as the air you breathe or your body as a bridge that connects your inner world with this part of your outer world. But each of your senses offers the same bridge, meaning that nature touches you through the receptors in your ears, your eyes, and your nose as you experience what you hear, see, taste, feel, and smell. You become part of the natural world, and it becomes part of you. It's happening right now. Like the river, connected to life within the water as well as what lies on the riverbank and beyond, you are interconnected to that which surrounds you.

The idea of nature interacting dynamically with your body can be a huge shift in how you may have thought of the natural world. Instead of your body being separate, this perspective fosters a relationship with nature based on your intrinsic connection to it. You may have conceptualized nature as a part of life that is labeled and categorized, existing as something independent from your existence; a landscape or sunset that you see but from which you feel detached. Using your breath and body as a conduit to forge a new and dynamic connection to nature is a significant first step in experiencing nature as you.

To take your experience of nature to another level, consider whether or not you engage with nature or simply observe. Even if your observations generate appreciation, do you still end up feeling distant and removed from what you are seeing? Engaging actively with nature is to have a felt experience of it. What I mean is that something inside of you resonates with what you are seeing, hearing, touching, or smelling.

Take rafting for example. It is entirely different to experience a river's rapids *on* the water than to look at them from above. In direct contact with the elements of a river, you go from observing to experiencing the river as the cold water splashes on your skin, and your muscles feel the jarring of bumping into a boulder. You and the river have merged at some level, in that you have a relationship *with* and not an observance *of* this part of nature.

But just in case you aren't a fan of river rafting, there are many more subtle ways in which to engage with nature. Think of how many moments of contact you have with the natural world every day. Imagine slowing down, practicing mindfulness, and noticing. You can start by paying attention to the ground as you walk, appreciating that the earth is supporting every step you take. When you head outside, really see the trees, feel the breeze, hear the birds, and smell the flowers as each of these displays itself to you. All of these can go unnoticed in a busy and distracted life. But if you do notice, and especially if you can stop for a moment, you are inviting engagement versus observation, closeness versus distance as you drink in your experience as a gulp instead of a sip.

As your relationship to nature deepens, you may discover things you did not know existed. You may start to see your judgment or your dismissiveness toward the natural world. Rivers, for example, are easy to judge or dismiss these days, with their level of contamination and clutter. So often the focus is more on which bridge to choose rather than noticing the body of water underneath.

Like in relationship to your body, what if nature could speak to you. Would it yearn to be known and appreciated for all the ways it supports your life? And would nature want to be acknowledged for its ability to restore itself in the wake of much that has been taken, like rain that clears the air and species whose numbers replenish when given a chance?

Your connection to nature based on respect and appreciation versus judgment or dismissiveness can foster a sense of an "I-Thou" relationship, meaning that we are equal to but not superior to the natural world. The powerful result of taking this stance shows up as a way of being in the natural world that not only respects and appreciates but also protects. Feeling protective then comes from connection versus only from a belief or value: from our heart rather than from our head.

A relationship with nature as we are exploring promotes humility and the realization that nature has something to teach us. There is even an approach to innovation that takes its lead from nature called Biomimicry. This approach seeks sustainable solutions to human challenges by emulating nature's time-tested patterns and strategies. The Velcro brand of hook and loop was invented by a man named George de Mestral in the 1940s while hunting in the Jura Mountains of Switzerland. Mr. de Mestral, a Swiss engineer, wondered how the tiny hooks of the cockle-burs attached themselves on his pants and his dog's fur. After studying the cockle-burs under a microscope, he went on to duplicate its design for human use.

My own recent experience is another illustration of a shifting relationship to nature and its place as a teacher. Not too long ago, as I have mentioned, I began living beside a river. I had no idea that my daily ritual of sitting on the deck and connecting with this alive, moving body of water would have such a significant effect on me. Each day my senses bring nature into my body. By staying present in the moment, I am aware of so much going on. I see a river that is home to lots of different wildlife. I see a powerful body of water that is ever changing and is affected by the ocean tides many miles away. I watch the dance between wildlife and humans – of humans emerging and wildlife retreating, only to reemerge as night falls and before day breaks. In the recognition that the same life energy sources all of life, when eagles, herons, and osprey offer me their beautiful display of flight, I fly with them. The same essence that radiates through my body radiates through theirs. Further, if I stay with what I am experiencing, I am awestruck by what I learn: birds that share dock pilings better than most humans share the planet, seasons that offer the wisdom of the cycle of birth and death, animal parents who display spectacular care of their offspring, and lastly, animal communities that work together in stunning reflections of true collaboration and nurturance.

As I wrap up this *Aspect of Wakefulness, Nature as You,* I strongly encourage you to change or enhance your relationship to nature. Start where you are and take it to the next level. Use your body to experience nature and practice mindfulness to notice what you see, hear, and smell. Adopt an "I-Thou" perspective that helps you drop any judgment you have so that you can see the wisdom nature offers. Mostly, I urge you to know nature as part of you and you as part of it, moving from a paradigm of separation into one of connectedness. In doing so, it is possible to experience the natural world in which we live in a whole new way, gifted by its beauty and aliveness.

I started by asking you to take a breath. I end with the request that you find what inspires you about nature. If you love waterfalls, go hang out with waterfalls. If you are moved by what you see in animals, find a way to experience them in their natural habitat. Even reading inspirational writing about nature can deepen your relationship to it. Poetry can capture the felt sense of nature, its essence, and its offerings. Here are two of my favorites:

*Ask Me*

> Some time when the river is ice ask me
> mistakes I have made. Ask me whether
> what I have done is my life. Others
> have come in their slow way into
> my thought, and some have tried to help
> or to hurt: ask me what difference
> their strongest love or hate has made.
> I will listen to what you say.
> You and I can turn and look
> at the silent river and wait. We know
> the current is there, hidden; and there
> are comings and goings from miles away
> that hold the stillness exactly before us.
> What the river says, that is what I say.
>
> William Stafford

*God's Creed*

> Forgive me that I cannot kneel
> And worship in this pew,
> For I have knelt in western dawns,
> When the stars were large and few,
> And the only fonts God gave me were
> The deep leaves filled with dew
>
> Ella Higginson

*Practice*

Below are some ideas to help you feel nature as you:

1.  If you can, go outside. Let nature touch you, right here, right
    now. Notice it, and when thought and mind arise, gently turn

your attention to the sensations, such as the wind on your skin, the sounds that you hear, and the colors that you see.

2. Do something you have never done before in nature, such as go to a natural hot spring, learn to camp, or even bathe in a stream or swim in the ocean.

3. Challenge your ideas of beauty by purposely connecting with a part of the natural environment that has in the past seemed ugly, disgusting (like connecting with snails or spiders), or just less than beautiful, such as putting yourself in a desert climate if you love lushness.

4. Check out nature-based spirituality, such as Nature Religion.

5. Prepare a meal from nature and give thanks to the plant or animal that is giving up its life for you.

6. Challenge your story about the weather; run in the rain, garden in the cold, find beauty in the clouds. As you have direct experience of nature, see if your story drops away. Are you really cold, or have you associated coldness with this moment? Is it really that difficult to hike in calf-high mud? Maybe. But maybe not.

7. Pick up one piece of litter every day.

8. Listen to "Ordinary Day" by Sarah McLachlan.

*Stories from the field* . . .

Hugh probably wasn't an environmentalist — at least not in a big "this is who I am" kind of way. He was a county social worker and the father of five daughters. He was a somewhat shy man, such that you wouldn't see him out as a social activist or standing on a soapbox proposing change. Though it was great for the environment that he walked to and from work every day, it had a lot less to do with pollution and a lot more to do with saving a few dollars every month on gas. But even with that, he noticed, enjoyed, and cared about the natural world around him. He would whistle while he walked, really taking in the sights, sounds, and smells he encountered. Typically, he picked up a piece or two of litter. Such a small gesture but one that made a huge statement: one person, one piece of litter; helping make the world a bit cleaner and more beautiful. In his quiet and unassuming way, he embodied and taught that we can each to do our part however big or small. From time to time I would accompany him on his walk. As he strolled along, he invited me to really take in the beauty and the sensory experience. On those walks, I did not hear judgment of those who littered, nor did Hugh attempt to pressure me to join in his daily ritual of litter patrol. He simply lived the idea of nature as part of himself, being a good steward along the way.

# Aspect Seven

## Conscious Relationships

Relationships, in their challenges and their glory, offer a fantastic opportunity to live as your awakened self. First, being conscious in your relationships means you've gained headway in not living as much in your ego (or at least you are attempting to do so). The powerful result is that your relationships are well served by others experiencing your awakened self versus your ego self.

Second, experiencing relationships as a part of your spiritual path can be transformative. From the gas attendant and the person driving in front of you, to your friends, family, and colleagues, as you interact with each person, there is the potential to see them in the same way you have come to see yourself, as part of something bigger. Like you, they are a river connected to the same ocean toward which we *all* travel.

The word "Namaste" offers this idea: "The God in me sees the God in you." Imagine what it would be like to have this experience with every encounter you have with another being. Imagine further how helpful this could be when you are dealing with someone difficult. If you can see beyond what is showing up on the surface, the difficulty will likely be less. And with less difficulty, you aren't as reactive and are more relaxed, which changes your whole demeanor. If you can stay tethered to the innate connection that exists, you might even feel a sense of freedom in not needing to "create" connection, knowing that the link is already there. Living wakefully arises without strain because it is our most natural state. Wakefulness in a relationship is no different.

So your launch into the waters of conscious relationship begins with your commitment to bring your awakened self versus your ego self to your relationships. It continues with the premise that you are already connected to others, innately. While this starting place can get us far in creating conscious relationships, some of us need more if we are to *stay* out of our ego and *remain* connected to others. Therefore, as we explore multiple components of having conscious relationships, I offer tools and ideas that help us go the full distance. Let's begin with one of the most important elements of conscious relationships: emotional regulation.

## Emotional Regulation: The Path of Peace

You've probably met people who are fully present. Maybe it is a friend, a family member, a therapist, or a spiritual teacher. I'm guessing that they were also noticeably calm. It might not have occurred to you at the time, but they were likely practicing emotional regulation. Emotional regulation doesn't mean that they weren't feeling emotions. In their company, you may have even seen emotions come up, such as joy, surprise, sadness, and perhaps anger. But their presence, their calm, was not compromised by those emotions; their ability to regulate simply meant that their emotions did not take over.

Practicing emotional regulation is a critical part of being conscious in your relationships and will help you show up as your awakened self: calm, present, and relaxed. Without regulated emotion, you jeopardize the ability for you and the other person to stay out of your egos and to feel the innate connection you have with one another.

When you are unregulated, in particular with anger, you trigger a protective response in others. Your unregulated anger sets them up to be in their ego because they will likely feel a need to protect themselves. That protection can take the form of unregulated anger on their part or a fast retreat. What comes with a protective retreat are walls of distrust. Remember that the ego gets involved when it perceives a threat. Therefore, living as your awakened self is not only about staying out of your own ego, but it is about engaging in a way that helps others to do so as well.

Given the effect of unregulated emotions on others, it's tempting to want to repress difficult feelings so that no one feels threatened. The problem is that repressed emotions have as many negative consequences as do unregulated emotions. One of the most troubling consequences is that eventually, pent-up feelings hit a tipping point, which in turn means that they are too big to regulate. A loop begins, whereby in trying to prevent unregulated emotion from happening through repressing your feelings, you set yourself up for the very thing you wish to avoid.

Even if your emotions don't explode later, avoiding them means that you have to work very hard not to feel. Not only that, it's easy to start resenting the other person when a part of you feels shut down. At the very least, both unregulated and repressed emotion can create distance in the relationship. So while the innate connection still exists, the distance keeps you from feeling it.

To get a sense of the impact of unregulated emotion, think of it like a wildfire. If left unattended and raging on its own, the blaze can cause great devastation. On the other hand, a contained fire can be a good thing. Real fires consume dead, decaying vegetation accumulating on the forest floor, thereby clearing the way for new growth. Some species, such as the jack pine, rely on fire to spread their seeds. The jack pine produces "serotinous" cones. The cones remain dormant until a fire occurs. Then the cones pop open, and the seeds fall or blow out. The fire is necessary for new trees to grow: no fire, no positive effect; an uncontained fire, potentially widespread harm. And just like the fire, growth requires that you feel emotions – without setting everything ablaze.

So know that feeling your emotions is not the same as having them take over. Your emotions, as wild and wonderful as they are, need your willingness to regulate them so that instead of creating damage, they serve you like a wildfire helps the forest over the long run. From the small provocation that can happen when you are driving your car in traffic to the big waves of grief of a profound loss, it comes down to your capacity to feel your emotions without being overcome by them. Sometimes the waves are big and long, but true emotional waves are never permanent. They come, and they *go*. They arise and then *dissolve*.

Anger is an especially important emotion to regulate, though being overcome by unregulated fear and sadness is served by the same process. Your best emotional regulation looks like this: First, you turn inward as you disengage temporarily from the other person or the situation until the emotion has subsided enough so that it is not controlling, overwhelming, or destabilizing you. You step away and internally allow your emotion its complete cycle, a wave that has a beginning, middle, and an end. You don't try to communicate because your ability to do so effectively is compromised.

Unregulated states make it impossible to access all parts of your brain, so taking a break is critical for allowing you to be empathetic and accurate in your memory. Thankfully, both remembering and empathizing are restored once we become regulated. This process can be as brief as 90 seconds or take more than an hour. But once the process has come to its completion, you are gifted with a sense of calm, able to empathize with your memory intact, and have better clarity. Too often it becomes clear that you don't have all of the information and are making assumptions. You are also able to be in touch with other emotions that were inaccessible to you when you are unregulated. Keep in mind what I mentioned in *Aspect Three, Practicing Mindfulness*, around the idea of working with inner pain. Those with complex trauma may experience emotional waves that last much longer and are not easily regulated without trauma recovery treatment.

In terms of anger, if you are in a situation that you can't leave, such as at work or in a confined area, still work with it internally. You might need to be silent or even say, "Just a moment" as you pause to regroup. If your anger takes you by surprise, realize that there were likely cues that went unnoticed. Signals such as a change in body temperature or growing impatience are indications that your anger is building. Knowing your cues can go a long way in working with your anger before it erupts.

The bottom line is that as your awakened self, living in the flow of your outer world, it is essential that you deal with your emotions. Emotional regulation builds on welcoming your emotions as part of you while ensuring that they do not sabotage your best intentions for having conscious relationships.

## Practice

1. Ask yourself:

   "How well do I regulate my emotions?"

   "Do I go too far and repress my emotions?"

   "Do I know when and how to self-soothe/calm down when I need to?"

   If you find answers that concern you, know that part of your journey involves working with either unregulated or repressed emotion.

2. Ask others how well they consider you to be regulated or repressed regarding your emotions.

3.  Find a safe and comfortable process such as journaling, or a person such as a therapist, to explore hidden and repressed emotions that may have been too much to feel before now. Having a process and especially having a person to accompany you can make all the difference.

4.  Reflect upon childhood influences in terms of understanding your emotions. How were they dealt with in your family growing up? Were people allowed to feel sad or were they told they "Should get over it!"? Was anger expressed in a frightening way? Or was anger avoided, creating an undercurrent of tension? If anger, in particular, was not expressed directly in your family, was it expressed indirectly as impatience, sarcasm, or constant bickering?

5.  Consider doing an anger inventory from childhood to adulthood, including anger you have toward yourself, others, the world, and even God.

6.  Adopt a practice to deal with your anger; a step-by-step process is offered next.

7.  Check out Dialectical Behavioral Therapy, which can help with emotional regulation and distress tolerance skills.

## Working with Anger

- Go in instead of out with your anger. Focus on working with your anger internally first. By going inward, rather than outward, you will likely immediately begin to calm down.

- Keep it simple. Take deep breaths. Put your attention on your body as your nervous system relaxes and as the activated chemicals in your brain stabilize.

- Wait it out and try not to judge your anger. You may take a few minutes or even longer to calm down. Stay with your anger as a wave as it moves through you.

- Go deeper. Notice if there are other emotions or vulnerabilities underneath the anger. As other emotions emerge, stay with them.

- Explore self-expression. When you are on the other side of the wave of anger, consider what you need. Sometimes in working with anger as described above, there is no need to follow up. The anger has dissipated and is gone. But if there is something, such as setting a boundary or asking for clarification with someone, when the time comes, make sure that you are ready and that you can express your anger in a regulated way. Doing so allows the other person to hear you without feeling threatened. Plan to choose your words wisely.

- Even before you engage with another, check out any assumptions you have. Look closely at your projections and expectations. What really made you mad? Did this person make you angry or are your expectations or your interpretations what actually upset you? Going a step further, if failed expectations made you angry, were those expectations clear between each of you?

- Finally, be aware of displaced anger. Ask yourself if the anger that is showing up is really about something else, which can be hard to see in the moment. So often what or who we think is triggering the anger is actually not the source.

## Meeting Another's Anger with Love

Meeting another's anger with love, for many, seems impossible. Most of us are afraid of anger and might either run the other way or meet anger with anger. If you can bring love, not fear or anger, to the table as you engage as your awakened self, it is powerful, even though doing so is challenging. Whether we like it or not, welcome or fear it, anger is part of the human experience. When meeting anger with love can be imagined as a springboard to deeper intimacy, it starts to sound worth it, even when it might be intense and uncomfortable. Remembering that someone else's anger, just like your own, often contains relevant information that otherwise would stay hidden is important. Whether it is a boundary crossed, a misunderstanding that needs clarification, or other feelings that are crying out for attention, not only does anger matter, it serves as an opportunity for the relationship to be honest, authentic, and conscious.

Meeting anger with love becomes much more possible as you work with your own anger. Your ability to see the meaning and the vulnerability embedded in your anger translates to your ability to feel compassion for others in their anger. In the work of emotional regulation, and particularly with this emotion, anger begins to be understood as pain and an emotion that often masks many other feelings, such as sadness, fear, loneliness, disappointment, etc. When the other emotions are felt, and another's pain and suffering is evident, most of us feel compelled to move toward, rather than away. That moment, the movement *toward* anger, is magical. When met in this way, as a force of love, anger melts.

To get past the fear of harm that can come with being present with another's anger, I encourage you to have both internal and external practices to help you meet anger with love. Few of us had any role-modeling around how to deal with anger. You may be the first in many generations to transcend a "fight or flight" response. To do so, you will need to have resources. It is also essential that you have a clear path so that your fear does not take over in the moment.

Below are ideas to help you turn the *idea* of meeting anger with love into your lived reality.

## Internal Practices

- Commit to your own anger work using the practice outlined in the previous section or by developing your own.

- Shift your mindset if you need to. Though it is uncomfortable, anger is a good thing, not a bad thing. You can decide that it is not a problem when you or someone is angry. Further, it may be about how they are expressing it, which means that the anger itself is not the issue. Try, if you can, to see anger as self-expression and self-advocacy, and part of a healthy sense of self. Imagine the alternative: the other person does not feel good enough about themselves to express their anger, speak their truth, and ultimately trust you with their honesty. See if you can step back and consider that the expressed anger reflects how much the relationship matters. Consider that this person, this angry person, may be showing you how much you and they matter.

- Focus on what lies beneath the anger. Imagine this person has a shield (their anger) with significant vulnerability on the other side of that shield. Picture how scared they are likely feeling and in that, the courage they had to muster to express their anger to you.

## External Practices

- Create ground rules for communication within the relationship. Ground rules often promote a sense of safety, and therefore, stronger engagement in the process. Good ground rules to start with are the commitment to emotional regulation, not using ultimatums, refraining from cursing, not making assumptions, and not overgeneralizing with "always" and "never" statements.

- If the other person is willing, connect with touch when processing anger. Honor boundaries, but if possible, offer a gentle hand on the knee or arm around the shoulders.

- Offer these statements: "Your anger matters" and "I am with you; I am here to listen" and consider thanking them for the courage to be honest and transparent with you. Express gratitude for their willingness to take the risk of your judgment or rejection and ultimately offering an opportunity for the relationship to deepen and grow.

- Practice receptivity as you offer your willingness to be accountable to anything you may have done to anger or injure this person.

- Learn from what has happened. Offer not only your availability in the moment but equally your interest in preventing further pain and suffering as you apply your learning to the future.

- Make sure that you stay current in your relationships, and for your most intimate ones, consider creating a regular time to check in. Having a structure, a defined time and place that supports expressing hard feelings like anger will help you and the other person do so more frequently. Taking this step prevents either of you from accumulating anger and improves your ability to express it in a healthy, productive way.

## Stories from the field...

I offer my story from the field, as working with my anger has been one of the most important parts of living as my awakened self. My unregulated anger did much damage in my life. I hurt others who then distanced from me. I created anxiety and angst for those I cared deeply about with just the possibility that I might become enraged. And every time there was an incident, I felt the shame, despair, hopelessness, and aloneness that came with the cycle. Initially, I thought that the answer was to learn to meditate, and meditation certainly helped. I thought if I got calm enough, I would *stay* calm. But there was a day that became a turning point, and I realized that I must do more.

It happened after a seven-day silent meditation retreat. I was to pick up my daughter afterward since she was staying close by. I left the retreat feeling deeply calm, happy, and connected to others and myself. It felt like nothing could shake me. Sadly, I was wrong. Literally, within 45 minutes of picking her up, I was throwing a Dairy Queen blizzard out of the window in a fit of rage. While I am quite sure she did something annoying, my unregulated anger was both uncalled for and sent me spinning into a state of anxiety, desperation, and disconnection: the opposite of my awakened self.

So in working with my anger, it became clear that I needed to slow down in *life*, not just on meditation retreats. It also became clear that I needed to deal with my anger better in the moment. In doing so, I had to learn to work with my body. I started by taking slow, deep breaths when I felt anger coming on. As I was better able to self-soothe, I began to see the assumption(s) that were adding fuel to the fire. I could also see that where there had been a betrayal or a boundary violated, my regulation allowed me to realize that my anger needed my voice, not my shout, to find resolution.

The deepest work I did, however, was to go to what sourced my rage. Facing my pain — in particular, my childhood wounding and the unworthiness that resulted — began to heal it. The more I healed and the more I claimed my intrinsic worth, the greater was my capacity to be and stay calm. Because my worth was no longer on the line, I was able to be accountable to others where I had hurt or frightened them. From there, I could sincerely offer my amends and atonement. Now I know anger as a dear friend, and as a powerful and meaningful emotional experience. I am grateful for how it has been a portal to some of my most profound inner healing.

## Practice Non-Attachment

The idea of practicing non-attachment in your relationships is about being more interested in a process rather than an outcome. This way of being is very different for those who have had a goal-oriented existence. The practice of non-attachment I am referring to is not about being detached *emotionally*. This distinction can be confusing, but it is crucial. Your awakened self *is* attached emotionally to others in the sense of feeling bonded. Practicing non-attachment is about shifting out of a linear, goal-oriented process with one goal in mind: in being open to multiple outcomes, you protect the bond with others.

Dropping your agenda and focusing on the process versus a preferred outcome can be tough, however, even though the rewards are well worth the effort. Our ego has driven most of us toward objectives that we believe we need or want. Goals met are not inherently a problem, and most if not all of us have enjoyed the results of meeting an objective. Only when an outcome achieved is great for you but not for the other person is it important to practice non-attachment.

In practicing non-attachment, your receptivity to multiple outcomes rather than being narrowly focused on one builds trust for others and offers them the experience that you are open-minded and flexible. Even something as simple as being open to a new way of getting someplace when asked by a passenger in your car offers that person a feeling of openness from you. Additionally, you may discover that the outcome that happened is favorable to the one you thought you wanted. In transcending your agenda, you may find something even better than what you initially preferred. In the example above, maybe you stumble upon a great restaurant along the way, one that you would never have seen had you insisted on your route. In the practice of non-attachment, while outcomes still matter, the relationship and the process start to matter more.

## Practice

- Ask yourself, "Am I willing to practice non-attachment in my relationships, focusing on process more or equal to outcomes?" Further ask yourself "Am I willing to face any barriers that stand in the way, such as working with my ego or overcoming distrust in the process?"

- Imagine asking a few trusted friends or a partner how they experience you: are you focused on outcome or process?

- Reflect upon what was modeled for you by your parents on the practice of non-attachment.

# Contribute to Another's Healing

Earlier, I invited you to look honestly at your childhood history, and how that history potentially meant you experienced pain, trauma, or loss. In living as your awakened self in your relationships, you can start to appreciate that the person in front of you has also had a rich and complicated journey. They may have gotten what they needed as a child, or not. They may know that or not. But what you can know is that there are powerful contributions you can make, whatever your particular offerings may be. Maybe it is communicating a bit more with a friend when you know that they hurt from a lack of communication with loved ones or easing up on teasing as a form of playfulness when you know that the other person has been teased in an unhealthy way.

Whether the nature of your relationship is romantic, a friendship, or a family member, the opportunity here is to bring sensitivity, curiosity, and compassion to each of your relationships around what your contributions might be. Envision asking, "How can I help you heal from childhood traumas, losses, or wounding?" Just asking the question is huge…a gesture in the *practice* of love, going well beyond *professing* love.

## Practice

- Lead with an appreciation that each of us has a complex and rich history that likely involves vulnerability in some form.

- Acknowledge within yourself and potentially within your relationships the role you may be playing in potentially triggering old pain. Offer sensitivity and a collaborative approach to working with an old injury being activated.

- Continue to heal your inner wounds as a part of being conscious in all of your relationships.

## Stories from the field...

Kimberly and Mark watched their childhood wounds dance and then damage the love that they had for one another. His extreme independence, as a coping strategy to virtually raising himself as the child of a single parent, and her deep loneliness, due to a sense of abandonment in her early years, was the perfect combination to create further injury with each other in their marriage. Her anger at his distance and his anger at her expressed pain did not have them heading in a positive direction. Until they could see that childhood wounds were being reenacted, creating disconnection and pulling them apart, the cycle continued. To the credit of each of them individually, first as a couple, and now, as divorced co-parents, they have turned a corner on this old dance. Their personal work in healing themselves as well as offering compassion and more in-depth understanding of one another's pain has dramatically reduced the number of times they find themselves in the cycle. And when childhood pain does show up, instead of reacting and distancing, they can lead with kindness and curiosity. Even though the nature of their relationship has changed, they continue to contribute to each other's healing.

## Practice Transparency

I have been using the idea of authenticity as part of your awakened self. Living with authenticity means practicing transparency. In this, there are two parts to explore: bringing your whole self to your relationships and speaking the truth. In terms of bringing your whole self to your relationships, I've never met anyone who doesn't like the *idea*, but being fully authentic means you let people see who you really are, which *includes* your imperfections and fallibility; basically what doesn't necessarily look good. And in terms of the *idea* of telling the truth, I've also never met anyone who doesn't like it. But just like bringing your whole imperfect self to the table, always speaking the truth can be hard.

As we have before, let's start with shining a spotlight on what living without a component of wakefulness is like; in this case, not being transparent. Without transparency, you hide from others, retreated behind walls, peeking out from time to time but mostly living with anxiety, distrust, and loneliness. At an earlier time in your life, those walls likely kept you safe. However, living behind those walls, along with the stress of keeping up appearances, likely becomes increasingly painful. Taking the brave step to practice transparency and live authentically involves facing your fears of living without the walls. For most people, the concern is the potential judgment or rejection from others.

In the *Introduction*, I shared some of the most painful history I have. To do this, I have to be at peace with that 200-pound suicidal girl in order to be fully transparent and let the world see her. I cannot control whether in reading that part you judged me. My ability to offer that level of transparency does not guarantee that I won't face rejection either. To practice this level of transparency means that I have to accept whatever the consequences of transparency brings, whether it is respect or disdain. In the end, it is my acceptance of myself that overrides any judgment you or others might have, allowing me to offer you, the reader, my authentic self.

My hopes for you are these: first, that living behind any walls that exist within you has become unbearable; that the sense of loneliness and isolation is not sustainable, no matter what the risk. I also hope that you are now more aware that your fears of rejection and judgment by others are a projection and that projections usually do not become a reality. People either don't judge or reject, or they are just too busy with their lives for it to matter as much as you think. But even more, I hope for you that in the rare case where you are judged or rejected, you know deep down inside that you can handle it; not only handle it but find a way that the experience might serve you. Maybe that looks like not taking it personally, and realizing that their judgment is about them and not you. Perhaps it is for you to strengthen your resolve to accept yourself in the mix of the rejection of another. It may be that it is time to consider saying goodbye.

The second part of practicing transparency, speaking the truth, is one of the most critical facets of having conscious relationships. It means you are not pretending, and that you say and reflect the truth. When someone asks you if something is wrong, you answer honestly. If you don't want to do something, you say it. Practicing transparency is essential, but in speaking truthfully to others, the when and how is also critical. Use your work on mindfulness to get a clear picture in discerning the when and how. Solid communication practices go a long way, especially for those worried about hurting or disappointing others. The following sections in our exploration of conscious relationships will help to make being truthful successful and rewarding.

As you practice transparency in all of your relationships, commit to hearing the truth from others as well. A willingness to listen to what is honest in your relationships is an incredible gift to every person in your life. Keep in mind that when you hear without ego, judgment, or reaction (regulating your emotions), you are offering receptivity to their experience, not necessarily agreement.

Your awakened self is free from the constraints of living out the old idea of who you are. Your transparency in the form of authenticity, truth-telling, and receptivity are precious facets of your awakened self in a relationship. The following reflective questions and integration ideas can help you bring your beautiful, flawed, awakened self forward!

## Practice

1. Personal Journaling:

   - What parts of myself have I not revealed to others in my life?

   - Am I different when others are not watching?

   - What information and secrets do I carry?

   - How do I feel about what I am withholding?

   - What am I afraid will happen if I fully reveal myself?

   - If so, are those fears real or imagined?

   - How do I feel about the prospect of sharing these reflections with others?

   - Is it essential for me to first look at my fears of judgment or rejection as I consider sharing more of myself?

   - Have I fully accepted myself so that any fears of judgment or rejection can be tempered by my self-acceptance?

2. Choose a person with whom to practice transparency. Consider letting them know what you are doing and that it is a compliment that you are willing to trust them. They will probably be of comfort to you as you contend with any uneasiness you might encounter.

3. Choose a situation, environment, or event to bring forth your most transparent and authentic self. As you ready yourself,

imagine any support you can offer yourself, be it self-talk in the moment or even a reward afterward.

4. Always tell the truth, no matter what. Imagine yourself creative enough to find a way to do it.

## Stories from the field . . .

Elizabeth didn't want to tell her husband about the affair. She said it didn't matter because she was leaving him, or was at least considering it. When I encouraged her to tell him, regardless of whether or not she stayed in the marriage, she thought I was nuts. I told her that her lack of transparency involved a secret that she would always carry. I suggested that carrying a secret and the shame around it had the potential to affect her relationship with herself significantly. I also offered that her secretiveness could poison any future intimate involvement in the form of a pattern of infidelity that might continue to play out. Patterns, I reminded her, are best changed by accountability.

Understandably it was hard to take in my perspective. Elizabeth believed that even if she chose to stay, telling her husband would only hurt him, rendering the choice both unnecessary and unkind. In a subsequent phone conversation, she shared her conflicted feelings. She didn't want the dishonesty, the shame, the carefulness that a secret brings, but she also didn't want to face the fear and didn't want to injure her husband further. I remained respectful of her choice and steadfast in my perspective. One week later she came in and reported something that for her was unbelievable. She had decided to tell him, and in doing so, they both got real and raw about how they felt about each other and the disconnection that they had *both* been experiencing. Between the tears and the transparency, a new level of intimacy was possible, what both had been seeking and missing for a long time. It changed everything.

I recently heard from her, happy in her marriage and the proud mother of two children that she and her husband had welcomed since the time I'd seen her. She'd sent me a picture. She looked glowing, and as I gazed at her picture, I could know and celebrate that her radiance was unencumbered by shame or secrets.

## Communicate Consciously

Floating back to two big ideas – relationships without ego and our innate connection to others – how lovely it would be to gaze at one another, enjoying the experience of connection without ego. But fortunately, or not, in relationships, we need to talk. Our gazing session is over when the time comes to ask for what we want, hear another's pain, schedule a meeting, coordinate date night or the soccer schedule with the carpool drivers, or even question why someone didn't empty the dishwasher.

Communicating can be hard work. Thankfully, in a way, *not* communicating makes for harder work. There are many pieces to put together in effective communication. Often, there are also bad habits to overcome. You are not alone if you feel like communicating well is uncharted territory. Growing up, perhaps your family members didn't communicate much at all, or expressed themselves in a problematic way, such as yelling or someone always needing to be right. Those experiences can be taken into adulthood, repeating generations of absent or poor communication.

The section on emotional regulation goes a far way in conscious communication. It can also be helpful to have a mindset that takes you a step further, a mindset that frames dialogue as a bridge that connects you to others on the human level. Remember that this bridge builds on the innate connection that already exists; it's as if communication makes a well-designed bridge beautiful and efficient.

My husband and I developed a model that includes a set of skills and powerful ideas for communicating consciously. It focuses on all parts of the communication process, from start to finish. We did this after years of seeing ourselves and our clients fail miserably at trying to communicate, no matter how well intended we were.

The model has three parts: Self Soothe, Engage, and Exchange. It is called the *S.E.E. Model* and offers a concrete process to follow. It remains a tried and true way of communicating that not only is successful but can be transformative. The *S.E.E. Model* provides a structure that creates a sense of safety and invites stable and continued engagement. Also, it can prevent both injury and repetition, as each person feels understood. Using the *S.E.E. Model* structure also promotes transparency. Though this model is a process, it ultimately deepens intimacy and helps you communicate as your awakened self.

Since communication is both verbal and non-verbal, the *S.E.E. Model* incorporates both. As you review the model, consider each part its body of work. The great thing about using the *S.E.E. Model* is that it reduces processing time. At first, it may not appear to shorten time spent, as there are multiple ideas and parts to the process. Given this, it is tempting to breeze over the first few parts and get right to the verbal part of Engagement. But don't skip over any part of the model, as all of the pieces are important to the process.

The first part of the model, Self-Soothe, which is about regulating emotion, is one of the most important parts of the process. It is worth repeating that unregulated emotion creates a stress response for the listener, usually canceling out his or her ability to hear and understand. For the unregulated person, not feeling heard or understood creates further escalation or giving up.

The second section, Engage, is equally important. There are four pieces to put in place in terms of setting the scene for a great verbal process. The first one, Leaning In, is about feeling a sense of accompaniment. For example, without a sense that you are with me, I might assume that you are not. The other parts of the set up further create an environment of safety and connection. For example, I encourage ground rules to be explicitly agreed upon, since, without them, we may trigger each other in the process. Ego work is crucial too, because if I let my ego lead the way, the process may be contaminated by competition, control, power, and potentially a sense of separation. Part of getting your ego out of the way is to accept that each person's reality is legitimate and stands on its own. In accepting dual realities, there is less a chance of arguing over "what's true or right".

Next comes the verbal part of the process and is the heart of it all. Each person gets a turn as speaker and listener. It is essential to use the model only when you have time for both. One of the most helpful things about this model is that any pattern of inequity in communication that existed before changes. When speaking, each person speaks from their experience, using "I" statements, and is asked to share at least two feelings. When listening, there are many elements with which to work.

In the model, I propose reflective listening; this is in contrast to how most of us listen: listening but at the same time preparing what we will say next. Reflective listening creates understanding because what is heard is repeated back...exactly. As the expressed words are reflected in the speaker's words, a sense of understanding and being understood grows. Reflective listening is not about agreeing with the speaker; the goal is to understand what is being said. What this looks like is the speaker completing their turn in an uninterrupted way as the listener reflects 3-4 sentences at a time, saying: "Did I get you? Is there more?" Though it may seem that a person would go on and on, the opposite usually happens. In an environment where there is no interruption, judgment, or self-referencing, people say what they need to say much more concisely and typically feel relief and gratitude for actually being heard.

In the listening process, once the speaker can say, "There is no more," the next step is to offer empathy, which invites deeper emotional intimacy. When empathizing, it is about connecting with the feelings shared versus trying to empathize based on relating to the speaker's perspective or experience. This concept is vital because we do not all share the same experience or perspective, yet we need to find a way to connect emotionally with others as part of conscious communication. Many have not thought much about the question of what true empathizing is. And while it is powerful to relate to someone's experience *and* the feelings involved, it is not always possible. Take the example of when one person is an addict, and the other is not. The person that does not struggle with addiction cannot empathize with being an addict because they have not had that life experience. However, if the addict breaks their experience of addiction down to certain feelings, such as regret, fear, sadness, and hopelessness, there can be common ground and emotional resonance between the two.

Finally, as part of the verbal exchange, the listener provides agreement, where possible, about what was expressed. If the listener doesn't agree, the hope is that defenses are not interfering, creating a "blind spot". But if what has been expressed by the speaker rings true to the listener, it is an opportunity to "own their stuff".

The last section, Exchange, involves a request and offer and provides a great finish. It often results in a sense of movement around a topic that might have been missing. Without it, you might be left with a feeling of "Where do we go from here?" The offer and request exchange can lend itself to resolution.

When using the *S.E.E. Model*, it can take multiple attempts to get through the full process. Try not to get discouraged. With practice, it becomes easier to complete. Remember that you and the other person are potentially changing life-long communication patterns, and it takes patience and repetition to create and sustain meaningful change.

In addition to the *S.E.E. Model*, I have also offered other communication ideas and practices. As with the *S.E.E. Model*, patience and repetition bring about sustained change.

## Practice

1.  Use the *S.E.E. Model* at the end of this *Practice* section. Print it off as a separate guide and keep a copy nearby. Know that many topics need several times of going through the process. Also keep in mind that each part of the process is a communication skill that you are building, as is the other person, and that it takes time to learn and use it effectively. Give yourself that time to attempt and reflect on what you and the other person can do differently when using the model in the future.

2.  If you experience a "miss" with someone, offer a do-over. Rewind and literally do a moment over again, like pausing and then rewinding on a tape. Your brain doesn't care as it learns new ways of being. Ask yourself, "Am I willing to offer a do-over? Will I say yes if asked for one?"

3.  Reframe what you see by considering if there is another way to see what is happening. Reframing builds on your practices for freedom from your mind from *Aspect Two, Freedom from the Mind* in terms of working with your thinking. Sometimes taking the long view versus a short view can make a huge difference. For example, if you are fighting with someone, a

great reframe is to consider how the fighting serves you, such as the perspective that although you are struggling, the struggle is potentially there to help you and the other person learn to deal with conflict better, such as setting ground rules or realizing that you and a partner need professional help. For anyone who has been avoiding or pretending, fighting is a good sign because it means they are no longer conflict avoidant. In this example, the goal, of course, is to learn how to deal with difficulty calmly and productively. The reframe is that conflict is not necessarily an exclusively bad thing.

4.  Lead with neutrality, or even better, give the other person the benefit of the doubt, assuming good intent on their part; this builds on your practices of challenging your thoughts from *Aspect Two, Freedom from the Mind*, as well as practicing mindfulness from *Aspect Three, Practicing Mindfulness*. See if you can stay present without getting too wrapped up in your projections. If you take in your experience from the perspective of just this current moment, what changes? What if you were neutral, or perceived the other person as doing their best and having good intentions? Always check out your projections; as you get clarification, stay open to a shift in your perspective.

5.  Consider asking the other person the following if you are stuck in your communication: "What do you need that you aren't getting from me right now?" You may find a breakthrough with just that question and the answer that follows.

# The S.E.E. Model

## Self-Soothe: A Great Start

Make sure you are calm as you begin, and focus on staying calm throughout the conversation. If emotions start to escalate, take a break, sooner rather than later. Agree together when you will return to the dialogue and do so as soon as possible.

## Engage: Set the Stage for Success

### Lean In

Communicate, "I am with you" through eyes, words, or touch.

### Accept Dual Realities

Shift from resistance to respect as you accept that each person's reality is legitimate.

### Get your Ego out of the Way

Your ego can show up as becoming defensive, needing to be right, over-talking, withdrawing, criticizing, blaming, or punishing as a way to protect against your fear. Name your fear rather than letting your ego dominate.

### Create Ground Rules

Establish ground rules to ensure a sense of safety for both people.

### Choose a person to go first and then switch

**Speaker:**

- Speak from your reality and experience.
- Use "I" statements and don't start sentences with "You"; this will help the other person stay open and prevents them from feeling accused or judged.
- Name at least two emotions you are feeling; be as vulnerable as possible.

**Listener:**

- Listen without interruption, judgment, or self-referencing (focus on what you are hearing versus thinking about what you are going to say).
- Reflect back every 3-4 sentences what has been said, in their words, and ask, "Did I get you? Is there more?" Listen until you hear "No."
- Summarize what you heard.
- Empathize around the feelings expressed.
- Provide agreement where you can about yourself or the topic.

## Exchange: A Perfect Finish

### Offer and Request

Individually make an offer and a request, based on what you have said and heard; this moves the topic forward, as well as encourages you both to ask for what you want and to practice generosity in your relationship.

## *Stories from the field . . .*

Their struggle was nothing new, but more intense because Bella's wedding was just hours away. Bella and her mom had always shared a deep bond, but that bond did not prevent a communication dynamic from developing over the years; a dynamic that too often left them both feeling bad, distant, and misunderstood. When they tried to talk, their attempts frequently made things worse. Far from a therapist's office where they might find support or a bookstore where a book could provide clarity, they were desperate. Behind their protective walls, each had a broken heart. On perhaps the most important of all days between mother and daughter, an abyss of pain separated them. The issue, from what I could tell, wasn't even insurmountable. It was the old dynamic showing up in the middle of this precious day.

I was new to my relationship with each of them, especially Bella's mother. A guest in her home, as I heard and saw what was happening, I was unsure what to do. I took a deep breath and gingerly approached. Though I did not have the *S.E.E. Model* in hand on a piece of paper, I had it etched in my brain. I offered to teach it to them, and they agreed, thankful to have a structure to lean on. And so, on a napkin, sitting at a picnic table and under a blue sky, I wrote it out. For the next hour, they put into practice communicating differently. What unfolded was more beautiful than the sky, as they really saw and heard each other. As the abyss became smaller with every passing moment, they got closer.

Their shining faces later that day may have been just as radiant without our afternoon experience. I sense not, however. The work Bella and her mom did is a testament to their love and their commitment to living and loving consciously. On that day, when there was no time to talk, for them, there was no option not to. Communication became connection and connection became a moment of healing. Later, Bella beamed as she danced with her new husband, perhaps heartened not only by the new chapter of her life that was upon her but by bringing her awakened self to it.

## Offer True Partnership

True partnership and the experience of equality are critical for living wakefully in a relationship. Feelings of inequity can erode the very foundation of the connection between two people, with distance that grows over time and resentment that can flourish. Back on the river, this would mean one person had to pack the kayak or is doing all of the rowing. In any relationship, an unhealthy dynamic can emerge when things are out of balance. Even between parent and child, while a parent does the lion's share of the work, hearing "thank you" balances what is given. For primary romantic relationships especially, it is about ensuring that there is a sense of fairness, from making sure each person has a turn to talk to delegating household, financial, parenting, etc. responsibilities fairly; even if they are not exactly the same, they are felt to be equal.

Though feelings of resentment are often your first clue that something is amiss, sadly, by the time resentment shows up, long-term patterns of unfairness often have been in place. It is not uncommon for these feelings to lay dormant and then dramatically rise once triggered. If you've ever found yourself saying or thinking, "You never do your part!" or "This is unfair," an important line has been crossed, possibly a few miles back.

If you and another person lack true partnership, regardless of the nature of your relationship, before approaching the other person, reflect upon your part. Ask yourself how you have contributed to the problem of imbalance, for example, "Did I ask for help with packing the kayaks?" or "Did I teach my children manners now that I am noticing a lack of gratitude?" Since typically *both* you and the other person had a part in creating the imbalance, *both* of you can have a role in re-establishing balance.

As you engage in re-establishing balance and equity, this includes your willingness to practice transparency and share the truth of any resentment you feel. Additionally, it is vital for you and the other person to explore any unspoken expectations or to clarify any misunderstandings. Where there is disagreement around what is fair, your next step is to move into a collaborative process. The next section, *Bridge Differences*, offers you a process you can use. I encourage you to start with the *S.E.E. Model* as a basis for understanding before using the *Bridging Differences Model*.

## Practice

1. Do an inventory of all of your relationships. Ask yourself, "Am I in true partnership in all of my relationships?" "If I asked others in my life, what would they say?"

2. Reflect upon your parent's relationship, and the overall values displayed. Was there a sense of equality and fairness in your family culture?

3. Define the meaningful contributions you make to all of your active relationships. Notice what you see; ask yourself, "Is it enough?"

4. Engage in a conversation about a true partnership with those you are closest to and see where it goes. The overall message is, "I am committed to doing my equal part" and the question to ask is, "What do you see?"

## *Stories from the field . . .*

Three eggs weren't supposed to turn into three babies – but they did! The triplets, Henley, Spencer, and Parker, joined their two-year-old brother, Steve, to make what was to be a small family addition turn into an epic change, in numbers and tasks. Joe and Emily had a good marriage but were still figuring out the basics of family life and being together when their lives turned upside down upon learning that Emily was carrying triplets. They were to be tested on many levels with the birth of their triplets, the least of which was their ability to be healthy partners in managing the extreme schedule their infants required while also attending to their other child and their jobs. They struggled at first with the common theme for many couples of "who does what and who has it harder" conversations. Joe and Emily's children all needed them and their work responsibilities pulled at each of them in different ways. Hard feelings like loneliness and resentment showed up. Though never directly questioning their ability to make it, the reality was that the lack of partnership was a very serious threat to their marriage.

Thankfully, something different happened. Joe and Emily figured it out, doing the vital work of forging a true partnership that replaced resentment with appreciation, and loneliness with companionship. By communicating, including a daily walk to connect and coordinate their lives, taking time together as a couple, but mostly by ensuring a sense of equality, they are better and stronger for this experience. Free of the distance that can build over years when there is a lack of true partnership, they have not only survived but are thriving, as a couple and as a family.

# *Bridging Differences*

*"If you want to go fast, go alone. If you want to go far, go together." ~ African Proverb*

As challenging as it can be, collaboration is equally as rewarding. However, when collaboration is compromise and compromise is a form of giving in, it isn't very appealing. But when collaboration through bridging differences is a win-win experience, without anyone acquiescing, it can be profound. Working together with another and finding "our way" as opposed to "my way" is truly living as your awakened self.

An example in my life illustrates the power of taking a collaborative approach. The topic was getting a dog, with two very different perspectives. With years behind us with multiple pets and at best, varying degrees of success, Gary did not want one. Though I experienced that same history, my life felt emptier without one. In the old paradigm, I would have controlled the process, and Gary would have given in. Instead, over two years, we practiced bridging our difference. We started with the practice of non-attachment; this meant that we did not know whether or not we would end up getting a dog. The next part of the process was to explore what we had in common, rather than how far apart we were. Without egos in charge by stubbornly taking a position, Gary could admit that he sometimes missed having a dog and I could acknowledge that life was much easier without pets. We had to hear each other's perspectives fully before we could find our common ground. Over time, discovering what we had in common led us to find an option that was right for both of us.

As you can see in our experience, we had to work with our egos, practice solid communication, and ensure a strong sense of partnership and equality, all of which made collaboration easier. A successful collaborative process is creative, and we were successful because we explored options with an open mind and heart. Hopefully, as you learn to bridge differences, you find yourself not only happy with the outcome but delighted by how you got there, without anyone giving in or engaging in a power struggle.

The *Bridging Differences Model* offers the step-by-step process described in the example above. Going through each of the steps is very important, especially the second step of finding common ground. You may be tempted to get right to problem-solving to find a solution. If you do so, you will miss a creative process that is connective and makes an initial difference that feels like a mighty river shrink to the size of a creek. Finally, outcomes are sustained more easily because there was meaningful involvement by each person, which is one of the best parts of bridging differences.

## Practice

1.  Start with a willingness to collaborate. Ask yourself, "Am I ready to find an 'our way' instead of getting 'my way'?"

2.  Reflect upon non-collaborative decisions you have made in your life. How did those decisions feel to each person and how well did they hold up over time?

3.  Frame collaboration as both relationship work, and as part of living as your awakened self. Remember that transcending your ego means not controlling a process or outcome. Remember also that your ego does need to feel included and not overpowered by another.

4.  Consider using the *Bridging Differences Model* on the next page and find a way to practice it. Like with the *S.E.E. Model*, print off the page as a guide.

## Bridging Differences

- **Clarify** each person's perspective and together define the difference you are bridging.

- **Explore** your common ground and discover how much alignment there is between you; this creates connections that might surprise you, such as values you didn't know you shared or areas of agreement that had not been seen. One of the first pieces of common ground can be that you both agree that you want to bridge this difference.

- **Create** as many options as you can that build on the common ground and incorporate each of your perspectives. Make sure to create more than one.

- **Pick** an option through a process of elimination. Remember, this isn't about getting your way; it is about choosing an option that works for both people. If you are having trouble finding or choosing an option, try this: go with an alternative that reflects only one person's outlook and try it as an experiment. Then, for an equal amount of time, switch to the other partner's perspective as an experiment. After you have tried both options, talk about what worked and didn't work to see if an "our way" emerges.

Getting stuck can happen. If you didn't find ANY common ground or an option that would work even partially, one possibility is to give the process more time. In the meantime, reflect upon your readiness to collaborate and work for a meaningful resolution.

## *Stories from the field . . .*

Peter and Dawn don't yell or fight. They never did. In fact, over time, they have learned to hear and understand each other better. They are both strong people, used to making lots of independent decisions. So while their communication was superb, there was a lack of collaboration between them. They realized that regarding important topics, such as financial partnership, they were afraid that in being collaborative, they would lose their sense of self in the process. Since most decisions were made independently, the result was a greater distance between them and on the important decisions, resentment for being excluded. Once in a while, when they did try to bridge a difference, they had a limited way of approaching it: identify the difference and look for solutions. For Dawn and Peter, collaboration work brought in the creative process; as they found common ground, they got excited to explore *multiple* options, not just arrive at a solution as they had done before. For them, this was huge. By integrating additional steps, they have gained a whole new dimension of decision-making. Instead of being afraid of their differences, now they look forward to a process that gives them their best outcomes along with a deepened connection with each other.

## The Deep Waters of Intimacy

### Emotional Intimacy

Doesn't that sound wonderful…the deep waters of intimacy? We have delved into emotions from the standpoint of regulation. Here, we explore the intimacy emotions offer. Like authenticity, I've rarely met anyone who doesn't like the *idea* of intimacy, but I've met many who either are afraid of it or have no clue how to create it in their relationships. As we explored in the section *Mindfulness and Relationships* in *Aspect Three, Practicing Mindfulness,* fear and discomfort are common. Thankfully, your awakened self knows itself to be innately connected to others. Adopting emotional intimacy practices builds on practicing mindfulness in your relationships. Emotional intimacy happens through emotional availability.

I define emotional availability as the freedom to express your emotions in a regulated way, as well as your availability to the emotional expression of someone else without feeling threatened, fixing it, making it about you, or shutting it down. Practicing emotional availability, given this definition, is a tall order, and warrants a deeper look at what can interfere.

Your relationship with emotions is vital here. In the *Aspect* on *Mindfulness,* we explored healing inner pain by befriending deep emotions from the past. In terms of ongoing emotional availability in your human relationships, it becomes about your *ongoing* relationship to emotions. If you experience emotions as far away, threatening, or inconvenient, it means changing your relationship to emotions.

As you take in that last sentence, and if the words speak to how emotions feel for you, it is important to explore whether it is about getting hurt, a lack of access, or simply being uncomfortable with the vulnerability that emotional depth creates. Your awareness around that discomfort is powerful information for you in terms of understanding your current capacity to be emotionally available. For example, if you tend to shut down your feelings, you likely have an impulse to do so with others as well. Perhaps you become aware that your resistance to emotions is about not trusting another's tears or feeling like you have to fix things when someone is upset. For some, being emotionally available is unappealing because it feels like offering support equals agreement with the other person. Resistance makes sense if emotional availability to another competes with staying connected to ourselves. The either/or choice of either I soften to you and lose me, or I hold back to protect myself, is painful and unnecessary. Practicing emotional availability does not mean being swallowed up by the experience of another.

As you invite a shift out of any resistance you feel, I offer ideas here, as well as more in the practice section. First, I encourage you to start with your mindset. Make the decision that you want to be emotionally available. Then, notice if you have resistance, perhaps as described above, or for a different reason. In the beginning, it is important not to judge or resist your resistance. Your job is to notice it and see what happens if you are curious. It would go something like this in your self-talk: "Wow, I am really resistant to my partner's emotions; I wonder what my resistance is about?" In asking the question, you will often be given insight into why it is hard to meet the other person's emotional experience; insights that can offer a path to overcoming any resistance to emotional availability.

The next step beyond working with your mindset is to explore ways that your resistance can be resolved. If you are worried, for example, about emotions that get out of hand, focus on communication practices, language, and emotional regulation. If you tend to fix, learn about practicing empathy instead, as well as adopting an attitude of holding people capable of experiencing their emotions and finding many of their answers. If it is as simple as you don't live in the feeling world, or have over-simplified feelings into the two categories of good and bad, consider a new paradigm where all emotions matter and can lead to rich and meaningful places when given attention. Attention can look like checking in with yourself multiple times in a day to see how you are feeling. If you are afraid that you will lose yourself in softening to the emotions of another, talk about it and practice internal boundaries. Internal boundaries do not result in a lack of empathy and emotional availability; you still care about the emotional experience of others and can show it. Having internal boundaries means, however, that in caring, you don't carry what is not yours.

The final piece I offer is to be opportunistic. Look for moments to put emotional availability into practice. Slowing down and tuning in to your and other's emotions can help a lot. We live in a doing/thinking culture, so feelings are often the last part of what is communicated. Instead of communicating on the doing/thinking level only, picture yourself asking, "How does this feel?" both to yourself and to others.

## Practice

1.  Journal about these reflective questions about emotional availability:

    *   What was your family culture in terms of emotional availability? Who showed you what you've learned?

    *   Do you know the difference between unregulated versus regulated emotions?

    *   Do you express your emotions, especially the ones where you feel especially vulnerable, such as loneliness, sadness, and fear? If you don't, when did the censorship start? How does shutting down your emotions feel in your body?

    *   What happens when someone is expressing his or her emotions to you? Do you try to fix something? Do you shut it down or try to avoid what is happening by changing the subject? Are you at a loss for what to do or say next?

    *   Does it make a difference if the emotion that someone is expressing is about you? In those cases, do you find

yourself feeling threatened in some way and then resistant to their emotional experience?

- Finally, ask yourself what it will take to practice emotional availability in your relationships. Are you willing and ready?

2. Put these practice ideas into action to foster your emotional availability:

- Spend time each day connecting and tuning into your emotions. If you don't typically express how you feel, imagine doing so, and see if you can shift from a paradigm of negative and positive emotions to the idea of having no categories at all, appreciating each emotion as meaningful and an important part of the human experience.

- Cultivate a practice, both internally and externally (with yourself and others) where you meet emotion with empathy.

- Working with your reflections from above, explore your expectations of emotional expression. Do you feel responsible for someone else's feelings or think you have to fix what is going on? Or do you hold others responsible for how you feel? Remember, offering empathy is often all you have to do. Being empathized with is often the best and only fix needed.

- Establish and enforce ground rules when expressing emotions. Good ones to start with are: not making assumptions, regulating intense emotions, and not interrupting each other.

- Slow down when emotions are present so that they can be fully felt and expressed. Taking a mindfulness approach invites deeper feelings to emerge.

- Consider asking the significant people in your life about their experience of you in terms of your emotional availability. Be receptive to what they have to say.

## Stories from the field...

Joanna was angry with herself for continuing to stay in what had become a functional and loveless marriage, and angry with her husband, Bill, for his retreating and lack of availability. Her anger masked the more important feelings that Joanna was feeling, which were sadness, hurt, disappointment, and loneliness. Then something powerful happened. In practicing emotional availability in her marriage, she realized that she had to start with herself. Joanna quit focusing on her dissatisfaction and began to connect with her pain and vulnerability, her sadness, hurt, loneliness, and disappointment; this meant sitting with those uncomfortable feelings and offering comfort to herself. In doing so, she began to heal, shifting away from blame and toward peace and calm. As her awareness of her vulnerability increased, so did her understanding of her part of what had unfolded in the relationship. Her whole attitude and posture toward herself and her husband softened. In that softening, he began to move closer to her again. As she is healing, so is her relationship. That healing began by accessing all of her emotions, rather than continuing to live in a state of anger. Bill is learning to access his deepest feelings too, and together they are enjoying a whole new level of emotional intimacy.

## Physical Intimacy

The power of touch is...powerful. When it is welcomed and safe, it connects us in ways that words cannot. In this section, I am distinguishing between physical intimacy and sexual intimacy. As an element of living as your awakened self, I invite you to consider practicing greater physical intimacy in some or all of your relationships. There are so many reasons why I make this invitation to you, but primarily it is because touch is a basic human need at all stages of life. Safe, physical touch relaxes our entire nervous system. It can help undo a sense of aloneness, deepen relationships, and create an intimacy that transcends what can be communicated in words. Imagine a friend who greets you with a hug, rather than just a hello, or a family member that offers a loving hand on your shoulder as you grieve, rather than just the words, "I'm so sorry for your loss."

In saying yes to physical intimacy in your relationships, you may be tasked with unpacking years of conditioning. For example, my schooling was such that I was strongly discouraged from engaging in any touch with clients. The ethics, of course, are to ensure the clients' safety, emotionally and physically. If I had chosen to adhere to this rule literally, however, hundreds of therapeutic moments would have been lost. When a client reaches out in gratitude to give me a hug for the work we have done together, my rejection of that hug would have disavowed our work. Even using physical proximity, and not touch itself, offers much in my clinical practice. I lean forward in moments of intense vulnerability for my clients; in doing so, I offer my physical presence. Over and over again my physical availability contributes to healing that could not have happened through words alone.

Looking at the physical bubble you live in – the felt sense of the amount of physical space from others you need – is a good starting place. Your bubble may be outdated, largely as a result of unresolved pain or unchecked projections. If so, you are kept from experiencing the power of touch and physical closeness. If you want to change that, your work in practicing *Aspect Two, Freedom from you Mind*, will help you to challenge your assumptions. Your work in healing inner pain, as described in the section *Healing Inner*

*Pain* in *Aspect Three, Practicing Mindfulness* will also contribute to your ability to practice physical intimacy.

As you proceed, do so thoughtfully and respectfully. While your physical boundaries may be changing, the boundaries and needs of others remain a hard line in the sand to honor.

## Practice

1. Ask yourself how much physical distance you need with others. If you sense that this is a way of protecting yourself, consider whether or not your protective wall is still needed.

2. If you have experienced physical or sexual trauma or violence, bring a seasoned therapist on board to help you invite physical touch into your relationships in a way that supports your healing.

3. Reflect upon ways to bring gentle, safe, affectionate touch into your relationships where it is welcome.

4. Have a conversation about physical touch in some or all of your relationships.

5. Challenge any assumptions you have.

6. Ask for what you want and be willing to hear no.

## Stories from the field . . .

Touch felt good to Garrett, but open displays of affection, especially extended affection, were extremely uncomfortable. There hadn't been any trauma or abuse in his background, and he and others around him knew him to be a very loving person. But the bubble around him existed. The effect of this bubble on his wife, Katerina, was sadness around the loss of physical connection outside of their sexual relationship. She was envious of other couples who were more demonstrative. As Garrett opened to the idea of pushing past his comfort zone, and especially in response to the sadness and challenge of this for his wife, he changed. He became more physically affectionate, not to a point where it felt inauthentic, but definitely past where he'd been. He became increasingly comfortable with extended touch; and while they were never going to be the most demonstrative couple on the planet, the change that did happen was more than enough for Katerina.

## Sexual Health and Sacred Sexuality

Now it's time to picture bringing your awakened self into the bedroom. In waking up, we come alive, and that aliveness extends to all parts of our life, including our sexuality. Our explorations so far – a loving relationship to yourself, intrinsic worth and belonging, challenging your thoughts and projections, and perhaps most importantly, having a cherished relationship to your body – may have had a positive effect on your sexuality. Or maybe you already feel wakeful in this part of your life. But if you struggle with your sexuality in any way, I invite you to dive into what keeps you from living as your awakened sexual self. And though human sexuality is complex, and deserves far more attention than this section provides, I encourage you to consider what I offer as a starting place.

Let's begin with exploring sexual disinterest, which has lots of potential influences. Changing hormones, emotional distance in the relationship, poor body image, or fatigue are but a few. Sometimes, what looks like sexual disinterest can be something completely different, such as in the cases where being unavailable sexually is due to an unwillingness to go through the motions, pretending, or not being authentic. If you are not as interested in sex as you used to be, no matter what sources your disinterest, it may be that the most important thing to do is first to ask the question, "Is sexuality a part of who I am?"

If the answer is yes, I encourage you to revisit resistance to sex with curiosity and kindness. If sexuality is part of who you are, even if you are not sexually active, it can be helpful to remember that shutting down any part of yourself has an impact on your well-being. Owning your sexuality and having gentle curiosity is a powerful step forward.

With your inquiry, answers, as well as options, will likely appear. For example, when your resistance is about hormonal changes or fatigue, the next step might be to work with your body. Maybe that means getting more rest or considering taking hormonal supplements. If your difficulty with sex is about your body image, change likely involves self-acceptance work. And if you relate to not being sexual because sex has become inauthentic or boring, it may mean redefining your sexual practices so that your authenticity is reflected in being sexual rather than avoiding it. The last example involves working with your partner. As your awakened self, and in practicing transparency, it is important to be willing to do so, even though talking about sex can feel daunting.

Imagine having a conversation about sex by exploring what "sexual health" means to each of you. You can talk about how sex may have changed over time for each of you and together, wade into the waters of how sexual health may or may not be represented in your current sexual relationship. Keep in mind that sexual health goes well beyond sexual practices and frequency. And part of sexual health is communicating about it honestly and directly.

For some, their lack of sexual interest is about the relationship itself. If so, there is a much bigger conversation to be had. And though it might be scary, it helps to remember the real consequences of avoidance: hurt, distance, confusion, frustration, and loneliness that can turn into doubt, infidelity, and divorce. I encourage you to read the section *Expressing Difficult Things* on page 171 to prepare and inspire you to approach your partner with relationship concerns.

Lastly, in our brief exploration of being conscious in your sexuality, I offer a final piece. Imagine what it would be like if lovemaking was part of your spirituality. As you have already redefined yourself as something more than your physical body, the essence of you connecting with the essence of another *through* the body makes sexuality an inherently sacred experience. Consider, who is making love to whom? Are the bodies of you and another the forms by which that sense of something bigger expresses itself? There are teachings and ideas about sacred sexuality that are available that I encourage you to discover. Here's a definition to start:

**Sacred Sexuality**: *Expressing sexuality in a way that goes beyond gratification and pleasure, with a presence of heart and mind to both oneself and one's partner. Since humanness is part of a larger whole, making love serves as a gateway to experiencing the Divine in ourselves and in another.*

*Practice*

1. Reflect on the following questions:

   • Am I a sexual being?

   • If so, does anything interfere with the expression of my sexuality?

   • Am I willing to do what is needed to shift any blocks to sexual health I discover?

   • How much personal or relational work around my sexuality have I done?

   • Does any unfinished work around this topic serve as a hindrance to a deeper and more fulfilling sexual experience? For example, body image work, infidelity?

   • In terms of sacred sexuality, am I open to a deeper or more expanded experience?

   • Have I had glimpses of what could be called a spiritual experience around my sexuality?

2. Experiment with your sexuality in the following ways:

   • Start with a connection to your spirituality first. Use mindfulness and body practices to deepen your level of presence in your body, and practice staying focused and not distracted when engaging sexually.

   • Slow down with your lovemaking and hold longer eye contact, slower movements, and a focus on sensation.

   • See or rent a movie that includes sexuality as a part of waking up and becoming more conscious.

3.  Begin the conversation with your partner on sexual health.

4.  Get help from a therapist if you have unresolved sexual trauma or find yourself unable to make the shifts you would like to make on your own.

5.  Find a book on spirituality and sex to read.

## Stories from the field...

"A great sex life" is what Lisa and Ben used to be able to say about their sex life. It was exciting, spontaneous, and connective. That was long ago. Now, sex had become routine, not very exciting, and infrequent at best. For both, though there was occasional frustration and sadness, the more concerning thing was that they had stopped caring. Not about each other. They remained, as they would say, "close". But they had stopped caring about sex by the time I met them. Years back, when they first noticed a change, they were alarmed. Extra date nights helped...for a while. They recaptured a bit of their old connection, but it felt forced. This new dynamic created anxiety, and over time, they returned to a place of complacency and neglect.

When we started working together, they had each resigned themselves to the idea that "a terrific sex life" was impossible in a long-term relationship. They didn't feel the effect of sexual neglect in their relationship because they had replaced sex with other things. She had begun a journey of personal work, meditation, and new ways of thinking. He had invested his energies into their children and his passions. But deep down inside, they were each affected. Though hard to admit, they no longer felt "in love". Both had experienced attractions to other people even though they had not acted on those feelings.

As they were able to access their buried feelings, they were deeply concerned. Without a change, they could see how sexual neglect threatened their relationship, or at the very least, created a glass ceiling around potential intimacy. But they were scared. They had tried to make a change before, and it backfired. So our work, in addition to practicing transparency with one another, was to help each of them reconnect with themselves as a sexual being. And on a relational level, they needed to be intentional but without a feeling of trying too hard. They brought in more playfulness and talked honestly about how a sense of adventure was missing. Inviting adventure back into the bedroom didn't involve anything crazy, but flirtatious texting and finding new sexual practices made sex exciting again. They explored bringing spirituality into their sex life, integrating mindfulness as part of their lovemaking. Now they have it all; a precious companionship in one another and a sexual connection that feels alive and sustainable.

## Heal the Hurts:
### The Powerful Terrain of Relationship Repair

Even in the most conscious, loving relationships, people get hurt. The harsh reality is that experiencing injuries comes with the territory of human relationships. Sadly, what is an even tougher reality is that too often the repair of those injuries and the restoration of trust in the relationship does not happen. Whether a hurt is due to a simple misunderstanding, or the injury is the result of betrayal, it's easy to try to "let it go" and move on without addressing it. The problem, of course, is that it doesn't go. As we have been exploring, when we get hurt, injuries have a way of sticking around in the form of distrust and walls that can grow and thicken over time. And when we injure others, the lingering effects can be haunting shame and ongoing self-criticism. Each person, then, is trapped in the past, which is the opposite of living in the flow of wakefulness. Wakefulness is about living in the now.

Part of the temptation to "let go" of what happened is having the awareness that most relational injuries are unintended. You didn't *mean* to cause pain. They weren't *trying* to hurt you. While giving yourself or another person the benefit of the doubt is an incredible gift, if the injury remains unresolved, there is no escaping the unintended consequences that can occur. At that point, our best intentions come back to bite us. Maybe it's a sarcastic remark that you find yourself making that tells you that something is still wrong. Perhaps it's the distance you feel even though the other person has reassured you that everything is okay. If you are avoiding repair based on good intentions, your work is to be willing to heal injuries proactively even if it feels scary and uncomfortable to do so. A great motivator is the understanding that if I resist healing current pain, I probably create more.

Working with the fear and discomfort involved in repairing injuries is a tall order; kind of like how you really want to get to the top of the hill, but the hike seems steep and difficult from down below. For most of us, we do not know what to do. There are those brave souls who have attempted to repair injuries. And for some of them, it has worked. Trust is restored, and the sense of resolution lasts. Forgiveness has been offered, and everyone has moved on. But many of us, probably the majority of us, have either avoided repair work or botched it up.

Just as avoiding repair can cause further injury, attempts to heal an injury without tools or a clear path can also create additional pain. Such as when someone tries to explain what happened, but what they say ends up sounding more like justification rather than clarification; this, in turn, can create another injury or at the very least, frustration. Or how about when you or the other person apologized, but doubt remained in trusting that the same thing wouldn't happen again? Finally, there are those times when an apology is offered, but it falls flat because it feels defensive rather than empathetic.

Certainly, you can give yourself gold stars for trying to do *something*, but if you are to continue to make attempts at repair, you must find a process that offers sustained resolution, renewed trust, and promotes forgiveness. My husband and I developed a repair tool that is focused on healing injuries in a way that results in each of these benefits. The process involves four parts: Hearing, Expressing, Amends/Atonement, and Letting Go. It is called the *H.E.A.L. Model.*

The *H.E.A.L. Model* is a two-way conversation, but a *one-way* process, meaning that you focus on one person's injury at a time. If multiple injuries need repair, each injury is given its own time and place to heal. Each injury deserves this. Using the model results not only in recovery from relational injury but creates a relationship that is stronger than before.

## Practice

1. Do a relationship inventory that identifies relationships where there has been injury, caused by you or by another.

2. Offer a repair process to anyone you have injured where doing so does not cause further harm.

3. Consider asking someone who has injured you to repair that injury. If they are willing, let them know what the process looks like for you and why it is important.

4. Study and implement the *H.E.A.L. Model* on the following page.

# The H.E.A.L. Model

## 1. Hear about the Injury

As the person who has injured another, start the process by listening to the other person's expression of pain and hurt. Remind yourself that this is not about agreeing with what happened or allowing yourself to be hurt in this process. Remember, repairing injuries is both a part of having strong and healthy relationships and also has a role in gaining true resolution. Remain calm, open-hearted, and interested, focusing on really understanding the other person's experience. You will need to regulate your emotions, refrain from self-referencing, and stay out of your ego.

## 2. Express Your Pain

Now, the one who feels injured takes a turn. Begin to express your pain in the form of the specific feelings you experienced in being hurt. Know that this is essential to healing. While following the ground rules established in the *S.E.E. Model*, make sure to *feel* your emotions as you describe them. Your job is to express and release the emotion around the injury. If you do so while simultaneously following the ground rules, you will be heard and fully understood. This is how you heal.

## 3. Amends and Atonement

Next, it is time for the person who has injured to respond. After hearing and seeing the expressed emotion surrounding an injury, lean in with empathy and remorse, offering a statement of amends. Even if you do not feel responsible for the injury, see if you can be sorry for the pain. Know that it is possible your defenses are keeping you from seeing your accountability. As you respond, try not to justify or explain what happened, unless you are asked to do so. Next, offer a statement of atonement, which means, "I am willing to do whatever I can to make this right." This step is a time for both people to brainstorm about what that might look like.

## 4. Letting Go

Finally, as the one who has been injured, consider letting go. Because a repair process has occurred, the opportunity here is to release what happened as a barrier between the two of you. Releasing what occurred can be very difficult. If this is hard to do, remember that we only hurt ourselves more if we carry old injuries. In letting go and forgiving the other person, it is not that you forget what happened, but that you remember what happened differently. As you make the choice to let go, return to that decision if you need to.

## Stories from the field . . .

"A wall of anger" was how it felt to Blakely. Years had gone by, but she could still sense her father's pain. Though things had improved in their relationship and fights no longer happened, the impact of struggle in earlier times lingered in the form of walls and emotional distance. Both Blakely and her father longed for the closeness they had enjoyed when she was young. Blakely began to realize that the closeness she yearned for meant saying yes to repairing the injuries that had created the hurt and anger. Blakely was brave. As she engaged in the process of repair, she brought her awakened self to the table. Hearing her father express his pain, she knew it wasn't about agreeing with what happened. She remained calm, regulating her own emotions. She did not interrupt and did not self-reference. By showing up in the way that she did, she opened up a space by which her father's tears could flow and his pain release. The entire process took perhaps 2-3 hours. The wall of anger melted and became a sea of gratitude and love. Blakely gave her dad an opportunity to heal and gave herself the gift of a path toward a restored relationship.

## Balance Autonomy and Togetherness

Conscious relationships include both togetherness and autonomy. Togetherness provides an important sense of security while autonomy ensures that you've not lost the "me" in the "we". Having both is especially true for intimate partner relationship but is a characteristic of all healthy relationships. Just acknowledging each as important can be, and feel, revolutionary.

As you explore how well you are balancing autonomy and togetherness in your relationships, look for any signs of imbalance. When there is a power struggle between the two, and they are experienced as an either/or proposition, there is likely imbalance. The goal is to have each person advocating for both. Emotions can be clues as well. Feeling resentful, like you're trapped or have you've lost yourself along the way, can indicate that you've not got enough autonomy in your relationship. Conversely, feeling detached, lonely, sad, or anxious can be the clue that there is not enough togetherness.

For each of your relationships, finding the right amount of autonomy and togetherness is where you go from here. In terms of togetherness, it is usually about having enough time together, but equally important is the way you spend that time, such that *both people* experience a sense of closeness and security. A classic example where there is time spent together without a shared sense of closeness is watching a sporting event or cooking show that is highly connective to one person but not to both.

In terms of autonomy, the specific amount needed for each of your relationships to thrive usually varies, with some needing more and other relationships requiring less. It is best to make the need and practices of autonomy an explicit thing and to know that there are many forms autonomy can take, such as solitude, time with a friend, and independent activities.

As you explore what togetherness and autonomy looks like in your relationships, the following practice ideas can help you create a balance between the two.

### Practice

1.  Reflect on what your parent's relationship showed you. Did they find a balance between autonomy and togetherness? Or did you witness a power struggle or only saw one or the other displayed?

2. Take some time to assess which (autonomy or togetherness) you are most drawn to; also notice whether or not you have resistance to either. If you do, ask yourself what the source of the draw and resistance is.

3. List all the forms of togetherness that create a sense of closeness for you. Likewise, list all the types of autonomy that you want to practice in your relationships.

4. Think about the clues that occur when there is an imbalance of too much togetherness or autonomy. Ask yourself if you are noticing any of those clues in your relationships.

5. Talk to those in your life about your reflections and insights. Ask the tough question of whether or not they are happy with the balance of autonomy and togetherness in the relationship.

6. Make any changes necessary to create more balance, and do so as an experiment or a "work in progress" kind of change.

## Stories from the field...

Jesse loved his autonomy and thrived in the sense of independence and freedom that he experienced. Pamela also loved autonomy, but felt alone in her pursuit of enough togetherness with Jesse, both as a couple and as a family. Before finding the balance of both, this was an area of struggle and pain in their relationship. Each polarized the other, and though they could both say that autonomy and togetherness were important, they were not focused as a team on what that looked like in their marriage. To experience meaningful change, they have had to get down to specifics in terms of time and activities. They've looked for cues of imbalance in finding the amount of each to get the benefit of both. It's been a process of trial and error, but they have kept at it, equally committed to the sense of individual freedom and a strong feeling of togetherness. Over time, Jesse and Pamela are finding their way. In doing this work, not only do they enjoy the benefits of a relationship that honors autonomy as well as togetherness but are contented by a relationship that is no longer caught in a power struggle between the two.

## Nurture Your Relationships

Envision floating downriver and seeing a beautiful garden on the shore. Imagine your relationships as that beautiful garden. Each relationship, like a flower, responds to your attention and care; conversely, each is impacted by neglect. Taking *care* of your relationships versus simply existing in each may be a radical shift. Just as your awakened self is self-nourishing, it is also nourishing to your relationships.

To begin, picture yourself gazing out at your garden, open to what you see. If you find signs of neglect, it's time to make a change, to get the watering can out, so to speak. This idea is pretty straightforward; however, doing so can look many ways, and can differ between each of your relationships. It can mean offering more time or better attention to others.

Offering more time can be overwhelming, however, if you already have a full plate. If so, adopt a mindset of quality over quantity, which frees you from having to come up with more time. Better quality time might look like being more present or choosing an engaging activity over a passive one (taking a hike versus watching a movie). These days, with the level of distractibility that exists as two people interact, your undivided attention is an incredible gift.

Sometimes, in gazing at the garden of our relationships, we see that it isn't the amount or quality of time that is the issue; it is about inconsistency. If this is you, a willingness to be consistent versus sporadic in maintaining contact is an immediate change you can make in nurturing your relationships. Consistency involves practicing true partnership in terms of equality and doing your part.

Now, I invite you to conjure up a few of the most significant relationships in your life. With each one, take a moment and sense whether it is nourished or neglected. If you get a sense of neglect, what comes next could be as simple as putting this book down right now and making a phone call.

Ultimately, your focus on this part of being conscious in your relationships gives those you care about the message that "you matter to me" and "we matter to me." And one of the best parts of developing a strong practice of nourishing your relationships is feeling content in that you have experienced with others all that's possible in light of the impermanence of life. You won't have to look back and wish for time you cannot recapture because, of course, eventually there isn't a later. Then, when it's time to say goodbye, you get to be grateful rather than regretful for how you showed up.

## Practice

1.  Do an inventory of your most significant relationships. Ask yourself these questions:

    *   What does each relationship need to thrive? Consider what the clues of neglect would be.

    *   Am I generally active or passive in my relationships? Am I two feet in and do I show up consistently, and if not, why? Do I expect others to do more than me?

    *   Is there anything affecting how I show up, such as a hurt that hasn't healed or an assumption that I am making? If so, am I willing to engage in a repair process?

2. Consider asking a few trusted others some of the questions above to get their feedback on their experience of you.

3. Be active by engaging in regular contact in all of your relationships, especially your most significant ones. Make the connection meaningful and consider setting up a ritual like regular dates (which are not for romantic relationships only).

4. Check in with the other person occasionally and ask, "How are 'we' doing?"

5. Explore what your parents showed you. Did they take care of their relationship and the other relationships in their lives?

### Stories from the field . . .

Claire tends to her relationships, and it shows. Like a garden, each relationship is watered and fed, with love and with consistency. Regardless of whether you are one of her children or her child's teacher, a new or old friend, a sibling or parent, a member of her extended family, or her partner, you can feel the sense of mattering to her. It truly feels like the warmth of sunshine. In her way of taking care of all relationships, Claire navigates family dynamics gracefully. With everyone, she accepts people for who they are and manages her expectations accordingly. She doesn't hold onto grudges and is deeply empathic when someone is in pain. And Claire shows up, dependably and with a smile on her face, despite her quiet, shy nature. She is present not only physically, but in the powerfully written words she offers from time to time. Claire reflects this element of having conscious relationships beautifully. Without being prideful, she is deeply proud of doing so.

# Navigating Stormy Waters

There are several areas of relationship that can be particularly challenging, especially from the perspective of bringing your awakened self forward. Expressing difficult things, asking for or being asked for change, practicing and honoring boundaries, and ending a relationship in a conscious way are a few of those areas. Below are some ideas and practices to help motivate you to venture forth with more confidence in your navigation. The payoff is significant, in that each and all of these areas, well traversed, have you living as your awakened self with others, regardless of how calm or stormy the water.

## Expressing Difficult Things

Most of us find it difficult to express difficult things, and some would say it is terrifying. Hanging out in tranquil waters can be tempting. Being conscious in your relationships, however, means that you bring it *all* forward, including the "hard stuff". The *S.E.E. Model* goes a long way toward helping get over the fear of expressing what is difficult. But if it still feels hard to do, and you have difficult things to express, read on for additional ideas.

To have your best experience in expressing difficult things, use your previous work in working with your thoughts and practicing mindfulness. Challenge any projections you have about the topic or the other person as part of making the experience a successful one. Confront your story if you hear yourself saying, "This will probably not go well."

In addition to using conscious communication practices, not making assumptions, and practicing mindfulness, go in with a positive image of the dialogue and remember the price of turning away from practicing this part of transparency: telling the truth.

Once you master expressing difficult things, you can imagine what it would be like to know deep inside that you could say anything to anyone. That's where these waters take you; feeling like a well-prepared navigator that can take on any conversation.

I have broken the practice of expressing difficult things into before, during, and after. See if you can integrate some or all of the ideas.

## Practice

1.  Getting Ready:

    *   **Prepare** what you have to say and **practice it** within yourself or **with another person. Be specific and concise** about what you are planning to say, offering a recent experience. For example, "Last weekend when I was struggling with my work, I didn't experience feeling supported due to your lack of time and availability" versus "You don't support me around work." As a part of your preparation, consider sharing what you are hoping to get out of the conversation. You may even want to have an outline for the things you need to say.

    *   Ask the person for a mutually convenient time and place, making sure that the place you choose is relaxing and appropriate for a more involved, intimate conversation.

    *   Address other stressors that could interfere with your focus, tone, and level of agitation so that you are as present, calm, and relaxed as possible.

    *   Use self-soothing and body practices to help you be and stay calm and centered.

- Practice non-attachment; expressing difficult things is a big first step for many of us, so it's good to let go of outcomes and focus on the process of saying what you need to say well and being heard without the other person feeling judged or criticized.
- Hold the other person capable of hearing what you are saying, and working through their feelings over time.

2. Diving In:

- Start with a statement of gratitude for the person's availability and their willingness to listen. Go a step further and offer reciprocity in hearing difficult things.
- Make soft and direct eye contact; lean in and touch as appropriate.
- Ask to be able to share without interruption; as you share, go slowly enough so that the person feels talked with, rather than talked at.
- Acknowledge that they may have a different perspective.
- Be truthful; don't sugarcoat, and don't repeat yourself.
- Allow for a response.

3. Wrapping it up:

- Thank the person again for taking the time
- Acknowledge any discomfort as normal and okay.
- Follow up with a gesture of kindness: a note, text, or small gift.

## *Stories from the field . . .*

Trent loved her. But not in the same way he had or thought that he had. Holding in the truth was breaking his heart, as much as it did to imagine having an honest conversation with Cathy around his feelings. He eventually summoned the courage to express what was difficult. He began with an image of a blanket of love enfolding them in their conversation. Though nervous, he kept going and was specific and clear in his message and intent. He had prepared the verbal part, which made it much easier to communicate his message in the moment, given his anxiety. Though difficult to hear, Trent's preparation and process made it possible for Cathy to listen to what he had to say. He shared his realization that keeping his feelings and concerns to himself was hurting him and Cathy much more than telling the truth. And not surprisingly, she shared that she had felt the shift and had been carrying great sadness and confusion over the distance between them. Without the expression of what was difficult, they were stagnant and in deep pain. By choosing, preparing, and trusting authentic self-expression, he got unstuck and started to live in the flow of his wakefulness. In expressing what was difficult, he discovered that although it wasn't comfortable, finding his voice was much easier than withholding it.

## *Embracing Change in Your Relationship*

As the saying goes, the only thing that doesn't change is change itself. This saying is true of relationships as well. Change is inevitable as each person evolves and develops over time. In a conscious relationship, the relationship welcomes and reflects those changes. A relationship that grows over time is exciting. When we are in a relationship that evolves most of us feel grateful and relieved because it means we don't have to compromise who we are to stay in the relationship. And what a prospect, as opposed to the opposite, when your relationships don't evolve with you. When a relationship doesn't adapt over time, it's as if you've outgrown a coat that has gotten too small. It used to offer warmth and comfort, though now you are increasingly constricted and uncomfortable. But instead of throwing the coat out, or living in discomfort, picture yourself asking for changes that you need. You might have to move on, but maybe not. And without attempting to ask for the changes you want or need, you'll never know. Asking doesn't mean that you'll get what you want, but *not* asking guarantees it.

The idea of asking for change probably sounds good. How about being *asked* for change? Does the idea still sound as good when you imagine being approached? Whether you are excited or resistant to this idea, it can be complicated, and thus often remains a buried hope and wish that never has a chance to come alive. Too often, a request for change is delayed long enough that it comes across as a demand. Demanded change, if it happens at all, comes with a high price. Usually, the change doesn't last, and there is a ton of resentment that can be felt by the person who gave in to the demand.

Therefore, it can be a remarkable thing to prepare for either possibility: to ask or be asked for change in a relationship. This is the path of practicing assertiveness and receptivity, both of which are part of living as your awakened self in your relationships. Below is a reflective exercise focused on being clear and prepared whether you are the one asking for change or the one being asked. Take some time exploring the following questions through inner reflection, journaling, or in dialogue with someone.

*Practice*

## Part 1: Asking for change

- Be clear about the change. What kind of change are you asking for: behavioral, relational, lifestyle, etc.?

- What are you hoping to gain from the change you are interested in making?

- Is this the only way to make that happen?

- How does this change you are asking for relate to your path?

- What reassurances can you offer that will motivate and encourage this person to consider saying yes?

## Part 2: Being Asked to Make a Change

When being asked to make a change, it can be helpful to break it down into three scenarios:

1. A change that you would potentially have made or want to make on your own

2. A change that you would be doing on behalf of the relationship

3. A change that compromises your authentic self in some way

The first scenario has the best chance of success. If asked for a change that you welcome, there is little risk of resentment, and it is likely to be a sustainable change. The person addressed it first, but the change is part of your path.

The second scenario, a change that you would offer on behalf of the relationship, can be trickier because the change can be less sustainable in light of the potential resentment you would have, and that it might not feel as right and good for you. If you can say "yes" to the request for change, it is essential that you have dealt with the part of you that might be resistant or resentful. Eventually, you will need to make this part of *your* path, not only as a loving gesture to someone. The result is a greater ability to maintain the change that you are offering to make.

The third scenario, making a change that does not feel authentic to you, is the most challenging and worrisome. In these cases, it is important to work the process through slowly so that you do not offer something that goes against your deepest sense of self or core values. Not only do you risk self-abandonment, but the change will also likely be harder to maintain over time and can create distance in the relationship. Consider the following before you head into the conversation:

- Is there another way to frame this request that makes a difference in saying "yes"?

- Can I offer this change being requested with a modifying request or as an experiment?

- Do I have an alternative option to offer and am I willing to be in a creative process to brainstorm options?

- If you have arrived at needing to say no, can you provide empathy and a willingness to consider this requested change at a later time?

### Stories from the field...

Abby was alarmed by Lou's drinking. She had asked him over and over again to stop, to moderate, to do something about a growing problem. Many promises for change happened after nights of binge drinking. Though the pledges came straight from his heart, he was unable to keep those agreements. The change requested was about his drinking, but coming from his partner, not within himself. He didn't like some of the consequences of his behavior, but did not see the problem as Abby did, and instead saw the important place alcohol had in his life. So she requested, and he promised to make changes. When he failed over and over again to follow through on those promises, she began to detach. Underneath her detachment was growing fear and aloneness. Finally, through deep work into what was sourcing his need to drink, Lou woke up. He realized that the trauma in his young adult life, in combination with his experience with his father, were both unresolved. In being unresolved, he had to drink heavily to keep the pain from surfacing. His courage to face his pain, and his recognition that his drinking was not the answer, allowed him to make a promise to himself: to abstain or moderate his alcohol use. Not surprisingly, he has been able to sustain that change because he is making it from the inside out and not on behalf of the relationship.

## Boundaries: Lines of Love

The previous section ended with a need to know where your boundaries are. What you can say "yes" to but what you need to say "no" to as well. This is part of having a strong relationship to yourself. Boundaries are like having the gear you need to protect you from over-exposure on the river. Without that protection, you shiver, exposed to the harsh elements. Not having boundaries when you need them is similar; your lack of self-care in this form may compromise your inner well-being. Maybe it is saying no when you need to conserve your energy. Perhaps it is setting a boundary as a result of being injured. Having boundaries in your relationships ensures your ability to bring forward your awakened and resourced self. Without healthy limits, you may find yourself bringing forth your tired, depleted, resentful self. And who in your life wants that?

A great way to start working with this part of having conscious relationships is with your mindset. As you adopt a practice of saying "no" when you need to, remember that you are saying "yes" to something else. Perhaps it is saying "yes" to self-care and self-love, to self-expression, to preventing resentment and staying resourced, to encouraging others to have boundaries with you, and finally, to holding others capable of working with any limit you need to set.

In addition to all of the good things listed above, once in a while, in setting a boundary, something better happens. Let's take a common example: being asked to help someone when you can't or it is best that you don't. Imagine saying "no" to a friend who wants help moving, only to hear later that the "perfect" situation unfolded. The person that helped them move was happy to have something to do that day. And this only could have happened with you expressing a boundary. In this kind of scenario, everyone is served. Everyone gets what he or she needs; without boundaries, not so much.

One of the challenges to prepare for is that in setting and keeping boundaries, you may anger or displease others. Allowing others to have their experience of your boundaries is a gift that you can give. What it looks like is this: you remain friendly and firm as you express a boundary and accept that they get to have whatever experience they are having. Your acceptance and ease not only helps you to remain present and relaxed, but it means that for others, you are not resisting their resistance. Know also that over time things may change. What is an initial negative reaction may shift to acceptance and even support over the long run. Whether they realize it or not, you are gifting them with your non-resentful self by maintaining boundaries. With all of this, you have an opportunity to stay out of your ego by being true to yourself rather than living behind the mask of pleasing others. I invite you to trust yourself and the process of setting boundaries as one that offers much to everyone involved.

If all of this is new territory for you, the first step is to make setting boundaries part of being conscious in your relationships. And whether or not this is a different way of being, I encourage you to explore the following ideas to start or strengthen your practice.

## Practice

1.  Reflect on your current relationships and ask yourself how well you set boundaries and how well you respond when others place limits with you. Go deeper and see what might stand in the way or what you are afraid of. If you notice a story, thought, or projection that is likely untrue, such as "My partner will think I don't care if I need to go to bed early rather than stay up and talk," use the work you did in *Aspect Two, Freedom from your Mind* to challenge your thought or story.

2.  Explore through writing or talking about what you were taught and shown in your childhood around practicing healthy boundaries. Was there support or were boundaries seen as selfish and shameful?

3.  Start setting boundaries. Begin to listen to and trust your internal voice that asks you, from time to time, to say no, honoring your boundary as a form of self-care and self-love. As you communicate your boundary to another person, here are a couple of ideas to ease the discomfort and help your boundary to be received well:

    •   Stay friendly but firm

- Offer empathy if it is a difficult boundary for them to accept

- Interact with soft eyes and ongoing eye-contact

- Make yourself available to brainstorm other ideas and options

4. Support others in having boundaries with you. Imagine saying, "I really want you to take care of yourself here" as you create an environment that makes it feel safe for the other person to say no. If you are having difficulty with a boundary that someone else is setting, acknowledge your feelings and experience, but remember the importance boundaries have as a keeper of well-being.

5. Finally, if you can, trust that if something is not happening in a particular way you want, then it is not supposed to.

## Stories from the field . . .

Penelope knew Michael needed to set boundaries with his daughter Nelly. Michael knew it too. He had been a single parent for a while, and as many do, had always felt guilty that Nelly had to go through the divorce. He asked too little and offered too much. And though Nelly loved it in the moment, she was beginning to suffer without the structure that proper boundaries create for a child. As Penelope and Michael started their life as a blended family, they knew that it was time for a change. Penelope knew that eventually, she would resent her stepdaughter without boundaries in place. Michael knew that he needed to deal with his guilt differently. Both knew that without these changes, they were in danger of this second marriage ending. Their household had started to feel chaotic and hectic.

Michael and Penelope started with one boundary at a time. They first chose to set a limit on availability in the form of "couple" time being uninterrupted; this was a significant change for Nelly, since she had always had unlimited access to her dad. But over time, she adjusted as she realized that her relationship with her dad was strong and secure. Parental limits around a consistent schedule and consequences to misbehavior were where Michael and Penelope focused next, resulting in a welcomed change in their home; no longer chaotic, their home and life offer a place for each and all to thrive. Michael and Penelope were thrilled to discover that boundaries created more, rather than less, love.

## Saying Goodbye Consciously

Living as your awakened self translates to living in integrity with what is true. In doing so, you may discover changes that are trying to happen in your life. One of those changes may be discovering that a relationship, friendship, romantic, or even familial, is no longer the relationship it was. Further, you may have arrived at the realization that it cannot be what you or the other person need and want. A painful realization in and of itself, the actual process of transitioning out of a relationship can be even more painful, so much so that many stay in a relationship far too long. It makes sense from the standpoint of not wanting to be hurtful. Protecting someone you care about from injury, or in the case where children are involved, wanting to protect others outside of the relationship, is a loving stance. But while the choice to stay appears to protect against experiencing pain, the choice to exist in an unhealthy, unhappy relationship is often more painful for everyone involved in the long run. As you live in the flow of wakefulness and your capacity to know and integrate the truth into your life grows, the question becomes not how to stay in a relationship out of obligation, but how to leave in a conscious way.

While Western culture does a great job of promoting strong friendships and romantic partnerships, it does little to show us the way in terms of a relationship ending. Because it can be uncomfortable and most of us don't know how to navigate leaving a relationship, it is tempting just to let the relationship slowly fade. Too often that involves saying we are busy when we could make time, or spending time together with a feeling of obligation and dread. Consciously ending a relationship is the opposite. It is to own what is true, what you want, and to lovingly make the change explicit with the other person. No easy task, but imagine that it is the most respectful and kind gesture to make, as opposed to avoidance or white-knuckling it. Imagine that like you, they can handle the grief experienced as part of letting go. And, like you, they may also feel relieved and grateful for getting out of something that's not working.

The topic of consciously saying goodbye is far too broad to capture in this section fully. But the seed has been planted as an idea that aligns with you living as your awakened self. In terms of moving beyond the idea, and where it applies to one or more of your relationships, the next step is to put it into practice. Know that resources exist, though the main focus is on romantic uncoupling and not around navigating the end of a non-romantic relationship ending. For that reason, after offering a few practice ideas, I have included two stories from the field: one reflects a romantic relationship ending, and the other a friendship.

## Practice

1.  Stay in your awakened self. Practice keeping your projections and assumptions in check. With decreasing contact, it is easy to make up and believe stories of the mind.

2.  Practice and support self-care. As you move through the process of change and loss, take care of yourself and offer what you can to support the other person doing the same.

3.  Go slowly. Your pain and adjustment will be best served with a mindful and thoughtful approach.

4.  Stay regulated emotionally. Bringing your regulated self to the process goes a long way in ensuring a positive experience for both of you.

5.  Where it does not cause further pain or injury, consider closure work, with each other or on your own; this allows for any pain and unfinished business to find a resolution. This step sometimes involves a therapist who has worked with change, grief, and repair.

6.  For those legally married, if you get stuck in negotiations, involve a mediator. Those in the mediation field can help you to have a "we" approach rather than be adversarial, and usually offer a family-friendly way of proceeding through the legal process.

7.  When uncoupling from a romantic relationship, stay open to friendship but cautious about being overly optimistic and moving too fast into a new relationship. Sometimes it is best to take a "pause" as a reset, so that when and if you engage in an active friendship, there has been time for healing and clarity.

## *Stories from the field . . .*

"In our friendship, we were adrift. Time together usually meant I was over-explaining why we didn't have more time together. My availabilities had changed, and when I was available, I was less and less compelled toward Jenna. We had enjoyed, over many years, an incredible connection. The combination of soulful depth and playfulness had been a rare and wonderful thing for both of us. As time passed, however, the dynamic of pressure, hurt, resentment, and incompatible expectations overshadowed that connection. I didn't want to end a friendship. In my life, it's just not what one did. You endure, you reframe, you hope for future change. But what I was increasingly aware of was that this wasn't working for either of us. My explanations were not reassuring. My availabilities were not enough. It wasn't that Jenna wanted too much. It wasn't that I was neglectful. It was the fact that over time, what we wanted and needed from the friendship was different. Jenna was the brave one. Our relationship ended when she sent me an email expressing her love and saying goodbye. I was shocked, impressed, relieved, and filled with love for her honesty and courage. I discovered an amazing thing; we could let each other go with love, something I had not experienced ever before. We could say goodbye, and in doing so, say thank you to one another. I will always treasure the connection and history I shared with Jenna, but even more, I cherish the dignity by which we let each other go."

◆

"I've been basking in the 'other' kinds of love in my life while my heart mends: with my parents, siblings, children, and even Debra, my ex-wife. When we first separated four years ago, I was lower than I've ever been, dangerously low, and practically lived at Katherine's office. I remember her inviting me to let myself imagine being healed and healthy again in my relationship with Debra. It was easy to answer that I would want to feel at ease around her again, with the jealousy, anger, confusion, and loss gone, and to be able to laugh and joke around with her still. It seemed impossible. But it has happened!

On my birthday last weekend, she invited me to stay for coffee when I came to pick up the kids. Her new partner Jill and all the kids were there, and we sat around the table for an hour telling stories. The kids read birthday limericks about me, my kids, and the others, and Debra wrote one, too. Then we went to my son's soccer game. Debra sat with Jill. Us hanging out, us being parents together, was a vision I could not fathom at the beginning. But as I moved through my pain, and we as a couple went our separate ways as consciously as we could, we have truly arrived on the other side. We are happy – or at least getting there – healthy, and have been able to show our children what love *really* is."

# Aspect Eight
## Finding Your Way in the World

Living in the flow of wakefulness is to live in connection to yourself, to nature, to those you are in a relationship with, and to all with whom you come into contact. But what about living in connection to your whole community and the world at large? That stretch, for some, is a big one. Whether it is about being too busy to engage with your community in a meaningful way or it is about having a lot of fear about the world at large, many people do not feel connected to what lies outside of their immediate circle. While it may seem that there is little consequence to living in that kind of existence, there are compelling benefits to making the stretch outside of your comfort zone: the benefit of feeling tethered to others who share the planet, the sense of trust that often accompanies engaging with those from cultures near and far, and ultimately, the benefit of feeling less alone in the world.

Let's begin with your sense of connection to the community that surrounds you. What I am referring to is not those that you know and interact with already. That is your chosen community. Instead, it is having a sense of connection to the whole community, and in particular, those who are different than you; this means connecting rather than co-existing with people of other races, abilities, or sexual orientation. Connecting with someone new and different may feel uncomfortable or even daunting to you. For some of us, even if we are open to the idea, we don't know what to do to make it happen.

Whether you are open or resistant, excited or scared, a willingness to move out of what is familiar is truly living the innate connection between us all, the innate belongingness referenced in *Aspect One, Befriending You*. Keep in mind that what is different is unfamiliar, and generally what is unfamiliar will always be a bit uncomfortable until you get used to it. By making contact rather than operating in avoidance, you are better able to break down internal barriers you have to others who are different, walls based on judgment and fear.

Traveling beyond your front door and past your comfort zone puts you on the other side of those walls and barriers, allowing you to see and experience the differences you resist directly. In doing so, "different" shifts from something superior or inferior, something to be judged or feared, to merely representing the diversity of life; this alone can be a significant change and invites you to see with the eyes of your heart. Stereotypes and beliefs often fall away as you have direct contact with the people and places you thought you understood. You transform by giving yourself firsthand experience. It is as if you become seasoned with delightful spices and ingredients that weren't in your kitchen cupboard, resulting in a much richer you.

Connecting with communities and cultures outside of yours can take many forms. Whether it is traveling to the other side of the world or the other side of town, either way, you potentially see something unlike yourself or the life you lead. When you see something new, a part of you is stimulated. Once that happens, you have a choice in what you do with what is new. Will you judge it? Will you back off from it? Or can you notice the unfamiliar with curiosity, inviting your direct experience to guide you? Choosing to be inquisitive and non-judgmental leaves you in a great position to decide what your experience means. No more stereotypes and assumptions, just your experience showing you the truth.

The potential is far-reaching. The gift of being seasoned and expanded by the differences you encounter provides recognition of what is universally the same between all of us. The connection we can feel with a gaze when language is unavailable; the helpfulness of a stranger when you have lost direction; or the way each of us are finding joy where we can, traversing the difficulties of life and making peace with loss. You get to discover the truth in the river metaphor I've been using, that each of us is truly like a river, unique in our human journey. And each of us, like a river, is finding our way to the ocean toward which we all travel. With an open heart to those you don't know and to those who are different than you, the sameness connects you, while the differences begin to enrich and inspire you.

I encourage you to turn those same loving eyes and open heart to those who are not as drastically different than you or do not live in an exotic, faraway place. Though a moment ago I encouraged you to look beyond your circle of people, now imagine taking the same sense of discovery back into your neighborhood, and to your circle of friends, family, and colleagues. What would happen if you engaged with what is *familiar* without fear, judgment, stereotype, or outdated information? Practicing a renewed curiosity, try looking at what has been familiar to you in a new way, putting assumptions aside, and seeing more deeply. You may be surprised by what you thought you knew and didn't and what you thought couldn't change but did. Your fresh eyes become the way to live in truth and accuracy with all who encircle you in life.

## Practice

1. Travel someplace new, close, or far. Slow down when you are there and take in the differences. Hold back judgment and keep your fears in check by not making assumptions or

projections. Though uncomfortable, see if you can stay present with what is happening and watch what happens when you do. If you can, do more than observe. Engage with what is different. Perhaps that means you eat something different or that you attend a festival that you wouldn't normally attend. Maybe that means you speak and connect with a stranger when you are in someplace new. If you can't think or access anything that seems different and unfamiliar, hang out in a public place or participate in public transportation.

2. As you notice differences, see if you can connect with what is the same. What do you see that you can relate to?

3. Take each of the above into your familiar life. Drop assumptions as you engage with new curiosity with your neighbors, family, friends, and colleagues.

## Stories from the field

Sara had seen the world before but in her explorations had always gone to places that felt safe and had only done so in the company of others. But Sara realized that though in traveling the world she was doing something expansive, there was a certain amount of fear that controlled this part of her life. Bringing her awakened self to her interest in traveling meant that Sara needed to do something different. And she did. She went alone, purposefully, and immersed herself in a strange and beautiful new culture. Her fears disappeared with each passing day, making this trip become far more than just her latest travel experience. Walls down, and with an open heart and mind, she transformed. Instead of observing a new place from a somewhat retreated posture while mostly engaging with her travel companions, she engaged fully with all of the people with whom she met, including her drivers, their families, fellow travelers she met along the way, and the locals. Though she went as a tourist, by adopting an attitude of curiosity and respect, she experienced the culture from the inside out. Sara's experience was possible because she faced her fears and traveled alone. Because of the depth of her experience, each new place and person became part of her in a way her previous trips had not offered. This experience has inspired her to face her fears and take her awakened self into many other areas of her life.

◆

Chloe lives in the world with an open mind and heart, relating to others without walls and judgments. She has traveled the world with that same openness to those she meets along the way. Chloe loves discovering new people and the joy of connecting with them. Her worldview is one of curiosity and trust, and she made a point to see the world through that lens. Now Chloe is home and in a place not so new. She is still herself: kind and non-judgmental; but in the familiarity of home, less intentional about how she is going to "show up" with strangers. Recently, at a local neighborhood market, Chloe and a friend noticed a senior woman on crutches carrying a heavy bag. She had no awareness that this woman was homeless. She and her friend circled back and asked the women if she was okay, given that she was having difficulty. The woman said she was fine but gratefully accepted the ride "home" Chloe and her friend offered. Much to their surprise, the woman directed them to a tent in the park nearby. She did not explain her plight in life, nor had a "song and dance" around her victimhood. She simply, with the same dignity offered to her, accepted the kindness of a stranger. Chloe experienced as much connection in that moment as she had in the many moments of meeting strangers abroad. This experience showed Chloe that by leading with the same trust, respect, and kindness embodied in traveling the world at large, wherever she is, Chloe can enjoy the joy and discovery of a powerful connection to others.

## Living in Troubled Times

One might say that times have always been troubled, that the human condition of violence and suffering has existed for all time. For some, it is worse than before. For others, it is better. For all of us, no matter what the relative amount of pain and suffering is in the world, what has changed is our accessibility to it. We see the effects of war, hunger, and natural disasters with live footage, often with images so vivid that it leaves nothing to the imagination. One of the most significant challenges in living wakefully is to do so amidst aggression and anguish in the world on a planet that is experiencing the devastating impact of climate change and political systems that seem unable or unwilling to intervene effectively and may perpetuate it.

If you are courageous enough to pay attention to what is happening, feelings of helplessness, depression, hopelessness, or chronic frustration can arise, as it can seem that you have little to no control. So much so that it can be tempting to check out rather than to witness and feel what is happening when you perceive that there is nothing that you can do. You might check out by becoming numb. The sheer volume and constancy of suffering and violence in the world, close to home or across an ocean, makes it easy to grow desensitized and detached over time. Or you might find yourself looking the other way and distract yourself, focusing only on your life and happiness, both of which are far more within reach to influence. Distraction offers the illusion that if you don't pay attention to the pain and suffering, it disappears.

But of course it doesn't disappear, and a part of you knows this. What is happening keeps on happening and some have to work pretty hard to ignore the trouble in the world. The question then emerges: Which takes more energy, smiling at a homeless person you drive by or looking the other way pretending you don't see them?

The choice to pay attention means you are living in truth and willing to contend with the emotional impact of what you see and experience. Doing so aligns with your awakened self, and means that you lean in, trusting your capacities to deal with life on life's terms. It is no different in this part of your outer world than trusting your capacities in your inner world. In deciding not to ignore it, the question becomes not "if" but "how" to bear the troubles of the world without compromising one's well-being.

Below I offer ideas to navigate these turbulent waters of life. My hope is that what I offer helps you turn toward the world with eyes and a heart wide open, willing to see the truth of what is happening and bear the heartache that may ensue. A great place to start is with your inner world and working with four ideas: internal boundaries, mindfulness, checking your projections, and changing your mindset.

As I described earlier, internal boundaries protect your inner core, allowing you to experience pain that is not yours without being swallowed up by it. It is the lived experience that another's pain is indeed not your own. You can feel it enough to empathize, but the internal boundary keeps you from carrying it. Doing this encourages you to be open-hearted rather than resisting another's experience because you cannot bear it.

Applying mindfulness when facing the troubles of the world is helpful. Remember that in practicing mindfulness, you don't shy away from what you are feeling in the moment. Your willingness to *feel* your heartache, your sadness, and fear, means that it can shift and results in you not *living* with a broken heart. In this part of the process, it hurts a bit more, but you do not repress your pain. Keep in mind that the practice of mindfulness is the discipline to stay in the present and not let your mind wander off into the future. What you are feeling, aware of, and processing is happening right now. In any given moment, that's enough with which to contend.

Beyond your discipline not to get lost in the future, it is equally important to refrain from making assumptions about what you see and learn. Whether you tend to minimize or inflate what is going on, if you can remember that you usually don't have all the information, there will be less unnecessary suffering for you. If you entertain projections, it's like you are adding fuel to an already blazing fire. The fire of the world is hot enough already; the extra gasoline of your projections only adds to your pain.

Practicing mindfulness and checking your projections does not mean being passive about what is unconscious, or not working to prevent pain and suffering where and when we can. It is about accepting that pain and suffering are a part of life. When you are truly present for the entire experience, it doesn't stop with the pain and suffering. I invite you to keep noticing what happens.

So many times, after a tragedy or in the presence of pain, something else shows up – eventually, some form of love. If you can be patient, and not look away from what is painful, see what unfolds. When we see only the initial unconsciousness in the world, it is devastating. But if you continue to watch what happens, see if what you discover is what I have come to understand: consciousness meeting what is unconscious, love meeting pain.

Love meeting pain is displayed beautifully in the form of human gestures, whether it is between individuals or gestures of global proportions. A cup of soup made by someone who loves you or a world responding to natural disasters displays that same arching up instinct that can cross even international boundaries with the message, "You are not alone. Your pain and suffering matter." Each of these is a message that can be huge in easing pain.

Now for the mindset piece, in terms of how you frame pain and suffering. Consider whether or not you resist the idea of suffering? If you do, as I did, it was before I looked more closely, and in doing so, changed my relationship and understanding of suffering. I began to see that sometimes, not always, suffering has a place. As I said above, this is not to condone acts of violence or neglect that result in suffering. More, it is to inquire in your life what the role of suffering has had and to imagine that same possibility for others.

Think about the role of suffering in how you have grown and evolved. Sometimes misery was what you needed to catapult you into a change that ultimately led to leading a more conscious life; this, of course, is true on a cultural, global, and environmental level. Change requires motivation, and sometimes, however sad a reality this is, motivation is catapulted by pain and suffering. Moving from a simplistic and exclusively negative relationship to the idea of suffering toward being open to it and considering an upside is a significant shift. However hard it is to make this shift, in doing so, you slow down your narrative that this or that "shouldn't" have happened.

Let's turn to a focus on your outer practices. One of the most valuable things to do in contending with difficulty in the world is to get involved in a meaningful way. As you engage, it prevents feeling helpless and promotes a sense of empowerment. For example, it may not be enough to vote. If I want the environment protected, for example, I buy land; if I am concerned about homelessness, I work or volunteer at a shelter.

Equally important is to take care of yourself, since when times are troubled, stress goes up. If you are not nourished and resourced, that stress compromises your well-being: your health, attitude, presence, and ease. Taking care of yourself can mean taking time to be in nature or limiting your exposure to the news and social media.

In the practice section below, I capture the inner and outer world ideas mentioned above and add a couple more. I encourage you to be hopeful about living wakefully in a troubled world as you consider turning some or all of the ideas into your practice.

## Practice

1. Lean into what is happening; feel it all the way through with internal boundaries well established.

2. Watch your projections and be committed to accuracy.

3. Practice mindfulness and living in the moment.

4. Change your mindset and relationship to suffering. Notice not only what happens but what follows, and the love, in its many forms, that meets pain.

5. Get active and make meaningful contributions to the world, large or small.

6. Practice self-care and monitor your exposure.

7. Find community and talk about what you experience of the world as a way to release it. Getting it out in this way can help it to move; not getting it out can lead to depression, desensitization, or disillusionment.

8. Engage with those activities that restore you, for example, books that inspire or movies that contribute to raising awareness and consciousness.

9. Listen to the song, "The Heart of Life is Good" by John Mayer or "Beautiful World" by Dierks Bentley.

*Stories from the field...*

Laurel is a spiritual teacher. Much respected and deeply loved by many, she walks the walk of living in the flow of wakefulness while living in the world. Laurel has not sequestered herself away to sit in the silence that she teaches. She lives, nestled in that silence in a world that is dynamic and difficult, troubled and transforming. After traveling the path of social activism in her earlier days, Laurel's spiritual awakening led her to a shift in how she sees and exists in the world she fought so hard to change. She has been able to take the long view, where before she did not understand suffering in the way that she does now. She can now see love meeting pain, consciousness responding to unconsciousness. A shift in her emotions helped her change; she feels things deeply but does not allow her feelings to overtake her or override her innate sense of joy. Laurel is not a woman who has given up recycling or is unaware of the world's affairs; more, she sits in the wildness of the world, doing her part, but free from having the troubles of the world tearing her up inside.

# Aspect Nine
## Exploring Your Spiritual Path

Much like the banks of a river that hold the water traveling seaward, a spiritual path can carry you no matter how difficult the terrain of life. For some, it takes the form of a particular religion. For others, a spiritual path involves a variety of teachings and ideas. One way to think of spirituality is that it is to have an individual practice that has to do with a sense of peace and purpose. It often means developing beliefs around the meaning of life and connection with others, without any pre-set religious values. That said, for many, part of their "spirituality" includes specific religious ideas or practices.

The most important thing is to have your feet on a path that works for you. If you already have what you would call a spiritual path, what I offer in this *Aspect of Wakefulness* will hopefully compliment what you have in place. However, if you don't have a spiritual path of your own, and if it feels necessary in living as your awakened self, this can be an exciting adventure.

A first step can be to explore some of the frameworks already available. Imagine heading out to a different church, synagogue, or meditation community once a week. You might hate it, love it, or be intrigued and want to dive a little deeper. Practicing spiritual curiosity with openness to everything throws the widest net. If you end up finding a religion or spiritual path that resonates with you, you get to join what already has form and structure.

Perhaps for you, the spiritual and religious pathways that exist do not fit. You have found that what is available doesn't have what you need or enough of what feels true and has personal meaning.

The more involved process then is to discover and cultivate your path. I'll offer three ideas to consider making your own as part of creating your path.

First is the idea of spirituality based on direct experience versus belief; the second idea is the possibility of your intuition serving as an inner guide; and finally, the concept of service as the embodiment of a spiritual path.

Spirituality based on direct experience is a powerful idea. It embodies what Gandhi said when he spoke of this: "I have nothing new to teach the world. Truth and non-violence are as old as the hills. All I have done is to try experiments in both on as vast a scale as I could." He is speaking of an invitation to join him in experiments with truth; this is in contrast to adopting spiritual ideas without any experiment at all, without your road test, so to speak, that offers affirmation. It is the same as what we covered in *Aspect Eight, Finding Your Way in the World,* around opening to those who are different by focusing on direct experience over stereotypes. Integrating this idea as part of your spiritual path then truly makes your path your own. Many spiritual concepts feel good and sound true, but to know something is true means you have your direct experience of it. It takes courage to do the experiment Gandhi speaks of in that you must be open to whatever you find, whether it aligns with your beliefs or not.

For example, if I believe that consciousness meets unconsciousness, something that sounds good and seems accurate, what do I find in my life experience? Are tragedy and suffering met with love? If so, then I can say "Yes" to the idea as I experience it as truth. Or, if I believe that there is no separation between myself and nature, what happens when I watch a sunset or look at the stars? Do lines of separation dissolve or do I "see" it without feeling part of it?

Staying vigilantly honest about your experience is critically important since, as mentioned before in *Aspect Two, Freedom from the Mind*, our mind looks for ways to confirm what we already believe and ignore the rest. Exploring direct experience versus belief means you are willing to see and accept *all* possibilities.

Using your intuition as an inner guide can also be a powerful part of a spiritual path. Your intuition is the voice of inner wisdom and knowingness, a strong, vibrant force that lies deep within you. The more you listen, the more clearly this voice can be heard. It is part of the boundlessness that you are. Listening to your intuition means that at times, your intuition goes against your logical mind, not making sense in the moment, and can even oppose what you thought you wanted. Bottom line, trusting your intuition and integrating it into how you navigate life means that you may not always like or understand what you hear.

If you don't relate to the experience of having intuition, it is likely you have not spent enough time listening for it. Or perhaps you haven't recognized the voice when it's been present. Once you hear it, I invite you to follow it. That involves paying attention long enough for you to be guided by what you hear. For most of us, at first, the voice sounds like a mere whisper, hardly detectable amidst the noise of the mind, and so is easy to dismiss. But your intuition gets stronger as it is given the space to be heard, especially as you learn to cultivate it. Asking, "Do I hear a voice within me?" "What is it telling me?" and finally, "Am I willing to trust it?" promotes an intuitive way of being. At first, this can be quite frightening; it can feel like turning your car over to an eight-year-old that has no driving experience with you sitting in the passenger seat trusting the ride. But your intuition isn't an eight-year-old. Your intuition is more like a wise 80-year-old with lots of life experience.

The more you practice listening to your intuition, the more you will be able to distinguish it from the voice of fear, optimism, or denial. The voice of intuition is a voice of knowing and feels very different. It comes to you as clarity without using your thinking to gain clarity. Your intuition can be more solid in a moment's time than the uncertainty that can exist after hours of mental activity. When you listen, you have privileged your intuition as a guide you trust. And like any expert guide, it is there to help you avoid dangerous rapids and to experience flow along the way.

The last idea to explore is service as a part of your spiritual path. As this entire book has presented, you are not separate from what lies beyond your body and your life. My hope is that in exploring and integrating all of the *Aspects of Wakefulness* I've presented so far, you are feeling generous and motivated to make a difference in the world. Maybe you were already feeling altruistic before reading the first page. If so, good for you! If not, perhaps this section of the book is the urging you need.

Acts of service are like little tributaries that connect one river to the other, reinforcing the innate connection we have to one another. What I am speaking to in terms of service goes well beyond volunteerism. It is a way of being in the world. It is as much seeing the disabled person in front of you and offering to hold the door, as it is hours at the local food bank. True service is not based on resisting the world as it is or gratifying your ego. Instead, being of service can be sourced from the sentiment, "my cup runneth over." As you wake up, something changes inside. The boundlessness that is you and the abundance that you discover in life creates a generous spirit. Service, then, is a reflection of generosity that unfolds naturally from living in the flow of wakefulness.

Perhaps the idea of service doesn't sound and feel good. If so, you are not alone. Acts of service can be driven by guilt and a sense of obligation, generating resentment that arises from feeling forced to do something good, making resistance to service understandable. And resistance in these cases is a good thing because it is a clue that the potential service to be offered is not coming from a healthy and generous place in you. So before engaging in service, it is best to work through any conflict, which could be as simple as giving yourself the choice or seeing that your struggle is because you have not been generous enough with yourself. It could even be that you haven't been creative enough about what service could look like for you. If you don't want to be in a cold warehouse for several hours, don't volunteer for a food bank. Consider being of service around one of your passions, such as if you love animals, helping at a shelter or fostering a dog.

Each of these three ideas – direct experience versus belief, intuition as your guide, and service as a natural result of living as your awakened self – make powerful contributions to cultivating your spiritual path. The reflective questions offered below explore what having a spiritual path means to you. The other ideas put your exploration of spiritual path into action.

## Practice

1. Journal the following questions:

   - What does spirituality mean to you?

   - Is there any resistance within you to exploring your path of living a more spiritual life? If so, where is the source of this resistance? Can you sit with the resistance without judgment or rejection, being curious and noticing what happens?

   - What would bringing a stronger sense of spirituality into your life look like to you?

   - Where has your intuition served you in your life? When were the times you ignored it, and what happened?

- How do you feel when you give? Does it come from joy, contentment, or gratitude, or a sense of guilt, obligation, or gratification of the ego?

2. Start each day with a commitment to listening more deeply to your intuition.

   - When you hear that voice, pause.

   - Notice your mind; does it dismiss what you are hearing?

   - Consider trusting the voice and following its guidance.

   - See if you can distinguish fear from knowing.

   - Circle back and reflect upon how well your intuition and its guidance served you.

3. Begin to look for opportunities to be of service, large or small. Notice how it feels and whether you notice any guilt or obligation. If you do, consider waiting to engage in service until you have a different relationship to it.

4. Visit a place of worship or a meditation community.

5. Ask people in your life who you experience having a spiritual path how they arrived at theirs.

### *Stories from the field*...

Mark is soulful and kind to others. Throughout his life, he has explored multiple spiritual traditions and practices. Mark does not define himself as religious, and even to call him a spiritual person makes him a bit uncomfortable. He would want to know what that means. Sometimes Mark wonders if he is doing enough to ensure that his life reflects his spirituality and his values. But what Mark can say with confidence is that he has chosen a path of living and loving consciously. He chose this as best for him versus joining a church or an ashram. Mark brings this idea of living consciously into all areas of his life, including taking care of his body, being conscious in his parenting, bringing greater honesty to his relationships, and being interested in making a positive difference on the planet. One of the differences he attempts to make is to be mindful as to the work he accepts professionally. Another is to minimize how much he consumes. He and his wife also toy with the idea of living off of the grid, such that they, with their son, can live a simpler life with less of the distractions and pressures of the world. For him, this is integrating his sense of spirituality and core values into his human journey. When you meet Mark, you can feel the depth and loving kindness he radiates as he lives as his awakened self, staying true to himself and the spiritual path he has cultivated as his own.

♦

Sophie couldn't follow her intuition at first. Leaving her relationship and contending with the impact on her partner, who did not welcome this choice, and the potential pain that her two young children would experience, was too much. She wrestled with her unhappiness for years but could not get past her fears and her guilt. She had heard the voice within her many times. It told her to leave, to quit practicing a form of self-abandonment, and to trust the capacities of her partner, her children, and herself to recover from the loss and find their way. At first, she ignored this voice within her. I remember the moment that something changed. It wasn't a mental process. It wasn't even one event, though several events helped catapult her into the ability to follow her intuition and make the very difficult choice to leave. Her story is an excellent example of hearing that intuitive whisper and becoming ready over time to honor it. She is still in the process of life unfolding from her ability to listen and trust. There is pain, there is the human journey of adjustment for all of them, but there is a level of living in wakefulness that Sophie had never experienced. In her words, she has never looked back, and even on her hardest day, she can recognize the good that has and continues to come from her brave choice to listen to her intuition.

♦

This story is one of life and death proportions, occurring within weeks of finishing writing this section on intuition. My husband and I were vacationing in Hawaii at the height of the big winter waves. We were excited to show our young grandchildren a bay filled with turtles so that they might see them since they were too young to snorkel. Gary and I had our snorkel gear on and were heading toward the familiar rocks where we had often stepped into the water. The waves were strong and getting in looked tricky, but there were many people in the bay, and the bay itself was calm. It was a matter of watching the waves and finding the right moment.

Gary proceeded to a rock that looked to be the best spot, with me right behind him. I am a strong swimmer, and I longed for the connection to the sea turtles I had enjoyed with each venture to this special site. I also wanted for my children and grandchildren to see Grandma Kath be brave, active, and engaging with life. Then I heard the voice, loud and clear, saying, "Don't go in." I paused, feeling conflicted and disappointed, and pivoted away from the water. I offered the sentiment to Gary, but he felt comfortable proceeding. I plopped down in displeasure, and I watched him out on the rock. After 15 minutes of gauging the waves, he was ready to go in. Then suddenly, a huge sneaker wave came up behind him. We shouted for him to get down, but it swept him over into a cavern between the rocks, pulling him under, and then a second huge wave kept him trapped. Unbelievably and miraculously, he was not killed by hitting his head on a rock or knocked unconscious and drowned.

I have never trusted my intuition so strongly nor have been given the gift of life on its behalf. Had Gary and I both been swept into the cavern, he and I may have experienced great harm. Without me in the water, he was able to climb out unencumbered. Had I been swept in, his instinct to help me, especially had I been injured, may have compromised his focus on himself, putting him at greater risk. By listening and honoring my intuition, it served us both.

# A Backpack Filled with Ideas

I have collected a few "big ideas" along the way; ideas that will help you live as your awakened self but don't fit neatly within the nine *Aspects of Wakefulness* we have explored. I offer them to you for your travels through life and encourage you to continue filling your backpack with your own ideas that inspire you.

1. Pay attention to when your expectations do not match reality. You most likely suffer when this happens. It is often the case that when reality and expectations differ, life is giving you a hint that your expectations must shift.

2. Meet small with big. If someone or something in your life feels "small" in terms of unconsciousness or being lost in their ego, try meeting that person or thing with a sense of your higher self, your awakened self: this might look like meeting unkindness with compassion or approaching competitiveness with collaboration.

3. Allow nothing and no one to have access to your nervous system without your permission! This is a wonderful mantra. As you practice emotional regulation, challenge your thinking, practice mindfulness, and have your sense of worth and belonging intact, the likelihood of being triggered lessens dramatically. It is a transformative moment when you can truly choose and not feel your sense of ease to be at the mercy of the world around you.

4. If you are having trouble in a relationship in terms of feeling stuck or flooded, you can do what I call "turning your process inside out." To do this, say, "I am feeling flooded [or stuck, or

both!]. I have no idea what to say or do right now."
Ultimately, this is part of the practice of being vulnerable.
When you lead with vulnerability, it often elicits a completely
different response from others.

5. Start a couple of daily practices. There are two that I highly
   recommend:

   - Say "thank you" for everything in your life. Everything!
     Doing so challenges you to find and see the goodness in
     everything. Ask, "How does this thing I don't like, am
     complaining about, or resisting serve me?" It isn't about
     apathy or not changing something; it is about starting from
     a different place.

   - Take a "love walk." Go for a walk and see how many forms
     and displays of love you see.

6. Trade in perfectionism for high standards. I playfully make that
   trade with clients weekly. It's hard to give up perfectionism
   when you believe that it is attainable and seems to produce
   great outcomes. But perfectionism is unattainable and
   stressful. High standards will do the same, in terms of
   outcomes, without the pain of reaching for something
   unreachable and unsustainable. I call it the 90% club. The 10%
   that feels imperfect, and is, is our bandwidth for self-
   acceptance and evolution. When life is happening at the 90%
   level, I can choose to accept my and others fallibility and
   imperfections. Further, in attending to do what is less than
   perfect, such as actively repairing an injury we have caused in a
   relationship, we surpass the 100% mark due to the intimacy
   and closeness created by the repair.

7. Create proximity to each person in your life that results in the greatest amount of love; this is what I call "The Proximity of Love." It involves being honest about the amount of time spent together, the frequency of contact, the geographical distance, and sometimes even the depth of how you engage; it is finding that line in the sand where you go from loving to unloving.

8. We have explored areas throughout the book where you may notice resistance. Beyond what I have already offered, I encourage you to know how resistance shows up for you, both internally and externally, which can look like boredom, restlessness, or tiredness, as well as irritability or defenses. Remember to stay out of judgment with your resistances and instead offer yourself curiosity. Resistance as a protective force is a critical part of your humanity; however, it can also override the consideration of making an important change or exposing yourself to something new and unfamiliar. Inquire gently within yourself, "What is the resistance about? Are my fears real? How can I support myself as I move toward something I am resisting?"

9. Live in integrity. Integrity equals alignment with who you are, what you want, what you say, your commitments, and your values. It also means honoring your inner feelings and experiences without dismissing or denying them. To get a stronger sense of this, imagine a mirror, one that beautifully and accurately reflects what is true within you, mirrored to your outer world. Living wakefully requires that you take a long, hard look at that mirror to see whether or not your authenticity is reflected. Once you make the brave choice to look, and then you see what you see, you will likely have some cleanup work to do. Even small ways of being out of alignment

still mean you are out of integrity. And if you are out of integrity, it matters.

Consider the following scenarios and how you would show up.

- What do you do when you have been given too much change back in a transaction? Do you make sure to return what is not yours?

- What about relational integrity? Have you offered transparency or do you gossip? If you don't respect gossiping and don't engage in it yourself, what happens when others around you are doing so? Do you join the conversation, or even more subtly, neglect to speak up?

- Professional integrity is also important. Are you showing up at work with authenticity? Are you showing up on time? Mostly, are you in integrity with yourself in terms of what you want to be doing in this area of your life?

10. Intention is a powerful part of living as your awakened self. Intention is what you aim for, like moving toward the ocean with the intention of arriving. But aiming for the ocean and getting there are two different things. You can intend to arrive without ever doing so, beached instead on a riverbank. Some people believe that identifying intention without a plan makes it happen. For others, there may be a plan of how to manifest their intentions, but they don't follow it. For some of us, it is easy to get stuck in identifying intentions and even our plan. Because we are sincere, we then camp out, feeling content, but don't do the hard work of bringing our intentions to life. Living your intended life involves knowing what you want, having a path to get there, and ensuring that you arrive.

11. Information is vital in helping you connect the dots of your life, making sense of things. Information can also offer powerful insights and clarity. But it has its limits. Many people think that if they have more information, things will change. Maybe you know a person, or perhaps it's you, who have naively thought that if you just understood nutrition and had a food plan, you would eat right, only to find yourself standing in front of the refrigerator eating a bowl of ice cream. Or maybe you thought that you only had to identify your childhood wounding for it to heal. Some seek information like it's a drug, convinced that once they have it, they will be okay. Sadly, this is often not the case. Information leaves you more aware, but not necessarily free of wounding or compulsions. So I encourage you to know the place that information has in your life while at the same time appreciating its limits.

12. Practice non-judgment in every facet of your life. Imagine it like taking the "should" out of life. Whether it is in not judging yourself, your body, those you know and those you do not, this is likely one of the most essential single elements of living wakefully. Judgment is innately divisive versus living from a place of innate connection. Judgment keeps you in your head, makes assumptions, and creates a relational distance that causes injury and pain, both for the other person, and you.

    Let's consider a radical idea: a world without judgment. It is probably impossible, but it is like imagining world peace. If we believe it is impossible, we disengage or at the very least, don't try as hard. If we believe getting closer to an ideal such as world peace or a world without judgment is better than nothing, we engage. And in doing so, we make a powerful difference in manifesting the world we want. A world without judgment is a world where likes and dislikes would be present, but where judgment and shame would not. This type of world is what you were born into from the perspective of you, the baby. You liked bananas and hated loud noises, but you didn't judge your sister for being loud, and you didn't feel judged when you kept your parents up crying. Of course, as an infant you did not have the capacity to judge, but practicing non-judgment is like returning to the innocent place of a baby; a set of eyes that sees the world with curiosity and awe; a set of eyes that sees yourself with compassion and acceptance as much as seeing others in the same way. This perspective is where you are going: experiencing yourself and life from the vantage point of having those eyes.

It's helpful to explore where your judgment came from to deepen the shift toward non-judgment. You are asking the questions, "Whose judgment is this?" and "Who judged you or who modeled judgment to you?" If you discover that the judgment you carry is not yours, it's easier to release it.

I invite you to also pay close attention to how it feels to judge and to experience judgment. When you experience judging something or someone, notice it. Pay attention to what is happening in your body, emotions, and your overall energy. Your ability to feel the toxicity of judgment can motivate your shift out of it. On the receiving end of judgment, notice all the same things. What is it like to have the experience of being judged? Do you go numb? Are you crushed?

So what is the medicine for judgment? What are you shifting into as you move away from judgment? As mentioned before, acceptance, compassion, and curiosity go a long way. Cultivating acceptance can look like adopting a "live and let live" attitude. Cultivating compassion means empathetically leaning into your and another's experience. In terms of cultivating curiosity, remember that you often do not have all of the information about a person or situation you are judging.

Finally, remember that being non-judgmental doesn't mean that you like something. When you give yourself permission not to like something or someone, it can help lessen a tendency to judge.

13. Accept duality in life, which means that you learn to accept two opposite things as both true and co-existent to one another; this is in contrast to fighting duality and having to choose one or the other truth. A duality I work with quite a bit with clients is living with the sadness and pain of the world's suffering while welcoming and celebrating the goodness and joy in their life. If you fight the duality, the pain of the world cancels out the goodness and joy. So instead, it is the use of the word "and" versus "but". I can be sad about the pain and still allow myself to be happy. Perhaps you can relate to this around losing a relationship. If it was a profound loss, you may have felt like "I can't imagine living without this person" but also, concurrent to that, knew you would go on. Both are true, and it is unnecessary to have to choose. Another example is wishing for a different body while accepting the one you have. Again, you can wish for a change and accept your body exactly as it is right now. Ultimately, when you accept duality as a part of life, it helps you stay relaxed because you are living life on life's terms. Life gives us multiple, distinct, and sometimes opposing realities; accepting duality allows you to be at ease. As you can see in the examples above, this idea runs through all *Aspects of Wakefulness* that we have explored. I encourage you to see how often duality is part of life and what living with "and" offers you.

# In Closing

I hope that as you come to the end of my book, you feel like you've come to the mouth of the river that meets the sea. It is not time for you to die, but you have perhaps had a sense of living more wakefully in your journey toward that ocean. In writing – and reading – this book myself, I come back to certain parts again and again. In that, maybe you get to go back upstream, integrating and reintegrating the ideas of wakefulness I have offered as you find yourself, the river, traversing differently because of it.

Five years from now I would write a different book, though the *Aspects of Wakefulness* would still be foundationally part of my journey. Maybe I would have them in a different order. Perhaps it would involve a few more stories. More likely, there would be more ideas in my backpack for living consciously, and my experience of living in the flow would have deepened. While initially frightened by the idea that *River to Ocean* would change over time, now it feels just right; the beauty of change as a reflection of the dynamic nature of consciousness.

Just as I have let my children go, embarking on their river adventures, I let these writings set sail in much the same fashion; filled with gratitude for the journey and the many gifts experienced along the way. In saying goodbye to a precious and dear friend, I trust that *River to Ocean*, like those who are so beloved to me, will find its way.

# Resources

If you or a loved one are concerned about suicide, contact the National Suicide Prevention Line at 1-800-273-8255 or go to your local emergency room.

## Anger

Hạnh Nhất. *Anger*. Riverhead Books, 2001.

Harbin, Thomas J. *Beyond Anger - A Guide for Men*. Da Capo Press, Incorporated, 2000.

Lerner, Harriet. *The Dance of Anger: a Woman's Guide to Changing the Patterns of Intimate Relationships*. Harper Collins, 2005.

## Anxiety/Fear/Stress

Altman, Donald. *The Mindfulness Code: Keys for Overcoming Stress, Anxiety, Fear, and Unhappiness*. New World Library, 2010.

Orsillo, Susan M., Lizabeth Roemer, and Zindel V. Segal. *The Mindful Way through Anxiety: Break Free from Chronic Worry and Reclaim Your Life*. Guilford Press, 2011.

## Authenticity

Brown, C. Brene. *The Gifts of Imperfection: Let Go of Who You Think You're Supposed to Be and Embrace Who You Are*. Hazelden, 2010.

Frederick, Ronald J. *Living like You Mean It: Use the Wisdom and Power of Your Emotions to Get the Life You Really Want*. Jossey-Bass, 2009.

Richo, David. *How to Be an Adult: a Handbook on Psychological and Spiritual Integration*. Paulist, 2018.

Strayed, Cheryl. *Wild: From Lost to Found on the Pacific Crest Trail*. Alfred A. Knopf, 2013.

## Challenging Beliefs

Katie, Byron, and Stephen Mitchell. *A Thousand Names for Joy*. Random House USA, 2007.

Katie, Byron, and Stephen Mitchell. *Loving What Is*. Harmony Books, 2002.

Katie, Byron, and Carol Williams. *Who Would You Be without Your Story?: Dialogues with Byron Katie*. Hay House, 2010.

Richo, David. *The Five Things We Cannot Change: and the Happiness We Find by Embracing Them*. Shambhala, 2008.

## Conscious Relationship

Gottman, John Mordechai, and Nan Silver. *The Seven Principles for Making Marriage Work*. Seven Dials an Imprint of Orion Publishing Group Ltd., 2018.

Hendrix, Harville. *Getting the Love You Want: A Guide for Couples*. Griffin, 2019.

Johnson, Sue. *Hold Me Tight: Seven Conversations for a Lifetime of Love*. Little Brown & Co, 2011.

Levine, Stephen, and Ondrea Levine. *Embracing the Beloved: Relationship as a Path of Awakening*. Gateway, 2002.

Real, Terrence. *The New Rules of Marriage: What You Need to Know to Make Love Work*. Ballantine Books, 2008.

Schnarch, David Morris. *Passionate Marriage: Keeping Love and Intimacy Alive in Committed Relationships*. Scribe Publications, 2012.

## Depression

Orsillo, Susan M., and Lizabeth Roemer. *The Mindful Way through Anxiety: Break Free from Chronic Worry and Reclaim Your Life*. Guilford Press, 2011.

## Parenting/Children

Hạnh Nhất. *Planting Seeds: Practicing Mindfulness with Children*. Full Circle Publishing, 2012.

Schab, Lisa M. *The Divorce Workbook for Children: Help for Kids to Overcome Difficult Family Changes & Grow Up Happy*. Instant Help Books, 2008.

Siegel, Daniel J., and Mary Hartzell. *Parenting from the Inside Out: How a Deeper Self-Understanding Can Help You Raise Children Who Thrive*. Perigee Books, 2017.

## Grief

Bernstein, Judith R. *When the Bough Breaks: Forever after the Death of a Son or Daughter*. Andrews and McMeel, 1998.

Bush, Ashley Davis. *Transcending Loss: Understanding the Lifelong Impact of Grief and How to Make It Meaningful*. Berkley Books, 1997.

Kumar, Sameet M. *Grieving Mindfully: a Compassionate and Spiritual Guide to Coping with Loss*. New Harbinger Publications, 2005.

Noel, Brook, and Pamela D. Blair. *I Wasn't Ready to Say Goodbye: Surviving, Coping, and Healing after the Sudden Death of a Loved One*. Sourcebooks, 2018.

Schuurman, Donna. *Never the Same: Coming to Terms with the Death of a Parent*. St. Martin's Press, 2004.

## Living/Working with Change and Difficult Times

Chödrön Pema. *Living Beautifully: with Uncertainty and Change*. Shambhala, 2019.

Chödrön Pema. *The Places That Scare You*. Shambhala, 2018.

Chödrön Pema. *When Things Fall Apart: Heart Advice for Difficult Times*. Thorsons Classics, 2017.

Lesser, Elizabeth. *Broken Open: How Difficult Times Can Help Us Grow*. Ebury Digital, 2010.

## Mindfulness

Hạnh Nhất, and Melvin McLeod. *You Are Here: Discovering the Magic of the Present Moment*. Shambhala, 2012.

Levine, Stephen. *A Year to Live: How to Live This Year as If It Were Your Last*. Thorndike Press, 1998.

Tolle, Eckhart. *The Power of Now: a Guide to Spiritual Enlightenment.* Yellow Kite, 2016.

Tolle, Eckhart. *Stillness Speaks.* Hodder, 2006.

Zinn, Jon Kabat. *Mindfulness for Beginners.* Jaico Publishing House, 2017.

### Spirituality

Brach, Tara. Radical Acceptance: *Embracing Your Life with the Heart of a Buddha.* Bantam Dell, 2004.

Ingram, Catherine. *Passionate Presence: Seven Qualities of Awakened Awareness.* Diamond Books, 2008.

Ingram, Catherine. *A Crack in Everything.* Diamond Books, 2006.

Ingram, Catherine. *In the Footsteps of Gandhi.* Parallax, 2004.

Ruiz, Miguel. *The Four Agreements: Toltec Wisdom Collection.* Amber-Allen Pub., 2008.

Singer, Michael A. *The Untethered Soul: the Journey beyond Yourself.* Noetic Books, Institute of Noetic Sciences, New Harbinger Publications, Inc., 2013.

### Recovery

*Alcoholics Anonymous.* Alcoholics Anonymous World Services, 1939.

Bien, Thomas, and Beverly Bien. *Mindful Recovery: a Spiritual Path to Healing from Addiction.* J. Wiley & Sons, 2002.

Littlejohn, Darren. *The 12-Step Buddhist: Enhance Recovery from Any Addiction.* Beyond Words Publishing, 2009.

### Trauma Recovery

Instaread. *The Body Keeps the Score: Brain, Mind, and Body in the Healing of Trauma* by Bessel Van Der Kolk, MD | Key Takeaways, Analysis & Review. IDreamBooks Inc, 2015.

# About Katherine Jansen-Byrkit

After obtaining a Master's in Public Health from the University of Washington, Katherine Jansen-Byrkit, MPH, LPC, started her professional work focusing on violence prevention and teen health in non-profit agencies. To her surprise, Katherine experienced an inner calling to follow in her father's footsteps and become a therapist. She went on to obtain her Master's in Counseling from Lewis and Clark College and then founded Innergy Counseling, her private practice.

Parallel to her professional journey, Katherine has also been on a spiritual path. At the age of 12, she discovered Transcendental Meditation, which she has continued in her adult years, including participation in silent meditation retreats. As Katherine began learning more from non-dualistic teachers, she began to see that her spiritual perspective and experience could be helpful for her clients. With that awareness, she started to offer ideas and practices of embodied wakefulness, including aspects of her own journey, helping her clients deepen their ability to live and love consciously.

Katherine now enjoys integrating the tenants of Public Health, principles of psychotherapy, and aspects of non-dualistic teachings in her work as a therapist, author, and teacher.

CPSIA information can be obtained
at www.ICGtesting.com
Printed in the USA
JSHW022129020819
1023JS00005B/17